for GENERATION

For information contact:

Ric Masten
Sun-Ink Presentations
37931 Palo Colorado Road
Carmel, California 93923

Tel: (831) 625-0588, Fax: (831) 625-3770

Ric Masten
www.ric-masten.net
ric.masten@earthlink.net

Library of Congress Control Number: 2005903601

ISBN -13: 978-0-931104-55-8
ISBN -10: 0-931104-55-6

Printed in China

Words & One-liners

Ric Masten

To Billie Barbara

CONTENTS

INTRODUCTION

Photograph by Cara Weston

Ric: Hard-of-hearing, one-eyed,
two-fingered writer,
hunting and pecking;
working amongst life's droppings
for *bons mots*
to tickle cerebral cells
into lifting eyelids –
better to see
the sight before them
before the end.

It's all true.

Masten and I have known one another for forty years, though our contact for much of that time was mediated by our common close friend Cook. Early on Ric gave me my first bead necklace. That was back when our Nation was fighting one of our earlier wars to promote Democracy. Ric sang and stood with Pete and Joan and many when it was so important for our Nation and the World. He got his ear pierced (I never went that far). Now he has a tattoo (this was a team-deed with his 25 year-old grandson). Just recently he offered me good counsel with a reminder of the old hippie wisdom, "Don't push the river."

In October, 2000, Ric mailed a fund raising letter to "friends, fans and acquaintances" seeking subscriptions to his first *Words and One-liners* book. The income from the book sales would help purchase the expensive herbal drug, PC SPES, imported from China, which he was using to fight his cancer.

Reading his letter describing the severity of his advanced, metastasized, prostate cancer – there is no cure – I responded with 100 bucks and a note containing the comment, "Ric, as near as I understand your medical situation, you're as good as dead."

Ric was overwhelmed (with giggling) by my pastoral prowess, and our relationship exploded into a remarkable friendship. We began by bouncing back and forth on the relation of "good" and "dead." Ric called it "pinging," as in Ping Pong. A near frenzy of correspondence took place for over a year.

From the beginning, there were arguments. One involved Ric's claim that in addition to his limited sight, hearing and typing skills, there were all the colleges out of which he had flunked, his severe dyslexia and his general dumbness. His IQ is 106. Who's to argue regarding blindness or dyslexia; but I did not go gladly with him down the pride-in-stupidity path.

Ric contended that people liked his poetry because they identified with his humble, uneducated dumbness. I thought his audiences and readers were attracted by Ric's unusual candor, honesty, wit, insight, stand-up manner, good writing, while addressing moments in life with which we are all involved – if we would but notice. I added to Ric, "By the way, at marketing you are not only not-dumb; you are near genius."

Friend Cook came up with the solution. Ric had discovered his IQ while breaking into his school's office to mess with his grades. He saw the IQ item. What happened, as Cook pointed out, is: Ric's IQ is really 160; his dyslexia inverted the zero and the six.

Ric never had his IQ re-tested, but his friends know what's what. He did fire his high salaried public relations director, and stopped advocating some common bonding power of stupidity.

Another argument was over his contention that I wrote poetically – a thought that had never occurred to anyone who had read my work. The thing is, Ric's sensory and cognitive limitations prevent him from

reading. Instead, he listens. He reads letters, essays, newspapers, books, e-mails, poems, obituaries out loud, so that he can first hear the words. Then he is able to connect the words together linearly for understanding.

So I tried his listening technique on my own stuff; went from listening – which soon included hearing the strange call of the Muse – to writing with rhythm, and started with the following e-mail to Ric:

the birds and the bees

The birds are
      two Old Birds
      chattering away the late afternoon hours
      on a park bench.
They met by chance
      after the war.
Now they get together
      rain or shine.
Chatting and remembering;
      muttering back and forth.

They discovered they had both been
      at Agincourt and Omaha;
      however, sharing wounds
      from the Tet Offensive
      came as quite a surprise
      ("You were there too?").
After that revelation,
      memories of Thermopylae
      and the Gates of Rome
      became commonplace.

"Hey, you're really beginning to look familiar."
    "Could we have been in the same squad?"

There is a haunting recall
    of a cave they once shared
    in the long ago
    which is foggy and unclear
    and still disturbs them.

The bees?

Well you know the bees.
    The busy ones.
    They build their nests,
    work all day,
    and are a lot smarter
    and more organized
    than most humans think.

I've mentioned several times
    the extraordinary ordinariness
    of our chatting.
Or would it be better said,
    the ordinary extraordinariness
    of it all.

For example:
    bees.

Who would have anticipated
    shared romances with bees.
Have all Old Birds
    had a bee time of their life?
Or is bee time just bee-ing human?

You want real extraordinary?
    Try this poem.

I can't afford
    to believe a word of it.

Too much at stake.

Whatever the writing's poetic merit, it's not bad for a beginner, and it sure was something different for me to do. Since Ric sent me his poetry all the time, now I could ping in on the fun. Ric bounced with me, along the path of writing, for months, now years, with steady walking counsel in the land of poetry.

Since 1968, Ric has made a living supporting himself, Billie Barbara and their four children, by being who he is – singing and strumming-to his own compositions. That doesn't begin to tell the tale of what he has accomplished with hammer, saw, level or with artist's brush. His ability to scavenger – get the right price – for building materials for his castle is without peer. The miracle he is pulling off medically, surviving advanced metastasized prostate cancer (and several associated conditions) – and now for years – is almost minor when seen in the panorama of his entire life drama.

Or, it would be minor except for the website, focused on prostate cancer, which Ric created and weekly maintains. The site is a gift of wisdom, medical acumen, careful documentation of medicines, procedures, as well as running along (skipping, strolling, and dashing, at times) with his repertoire of

Words and One-liners – old and new. The words of the website deal with matters of life and death, hope and despair. If you ask, he also will officiate at your wedding.

When the Polish poet Wisława Szymborska received the Nobel Prize for Literature in 1996, she said, in her address to the Academy, "Contemporary poets are skeptical and suspicious even, or perhaps, especially, about themselves. They publicly confess to being poets only reluctantly, as if they were a little ashamed of it . . . . When they can't avoid revealing their profession, poets prefer to use the general term 'writer.'"

If you ask Ric what he does for a living, he answers, "I'm a professional authentic person." That rubs me the wrong way. *Authenticity* is near the top of my list of the most important and desirable characteristics for a human being. I bristle at it being used promotionally or for show. When cornered, Ric says, "I only say it facetiously." I reply, "Then say something else. To the extent you're being facetious, you're not being genuinely authentic. Protect 'authenticity.' The world needs more expressions of integrity of character."

Then Ric adds, "But I'm also sincere when I say it. I really do just let me and my observations hang out there in the poems." And he is correct.

Billie Barbara wrote a marvelously succinct and insightful comment capturing the essential Ric: "All he wants from you and me is for us to listen to him." And I'll add a later comment of Billie's, regarding

both Ric and herself: "We are performers. That's what we do."

As you know – or perhaps you still are struggling with this learning – friendships involve real people, not pretend people. Friendship has a for-better-or-for-worse component. Ric and I have both been enriched by this knowing.

Abiding through all dimensions of Ric's character is his meaningful survival in the face of forces in life of an adversary nature, perhaps starting with his mother's effort at a self-induced abortion of him at eight months. Stuff like that kind of sets a tone.

I'm reminded of an observation by the photography artist, Diane Arbus, famous for photographing carny folk, bored suburbanites, dwarfs, nudists, transvestites, aging grand dames, as well as fashion photography. Critics often challenged her taste in subjects. Arbus, apparently, thought her subjects were human beings. She said, "Most people go through life dreading they'll have a traumatic experience. Freaks were born with their trauma. They've already passed the test of life. They're aristocrats."

Ric often expresses thanks for the conditions of his life, including even his cancer struggles. He feels he has been offered a lifetime – whatever the length – of enhanced hourly awareness.

It's also true that there is no way to ignore Ric's ego (for which he is almost famous). When he and I met for a first walk, about a year into our correspondence, we went to a favorite coffee café in my town. Within 45 seconds of arrival, Ric announced to everyone in the room, "My name is Ric Masten, and I am dying of incurable prostate cancer." As Ric sometimes says in his defense, "With me, you get what you get, no more, no less."

The next morning at the coffee house, the chat of the regulars shifted from sports, after I arrived, to, "I was afraid he might die halfway through his latte." Laughter. I said, "Ric is a poet dealing with death. He shares what he knows and learns." But the reply was coarse: "Bunk. He uses his dying to promote himself."

Nevertheless, that morning there was some discussion of death and dying; a topic never even approached before. Weeks later, one acquaintance asked for the address of Ric's website. He was nervous over his own lump which had just been discovered.

Lorna and I visited with Ric (and Billie Barbara) at the San Francisco Medical Center where he had hip replacement surgery. A couple of incidents had preceded the surgery.

The logistics of getting Ric to the surgery from his home in Big Sur also involved lugging a couple hundred pounds of his books. I had suggested leaving the books home. Ric did not take well to that. He evaluates the medical establishment by whether or not his poetry is liked. Good doctors like it. They, as well as nurses and hospital personnel, are rewarded with autographed copies. He's pretty obstinate expounding

and defending his standard of excellence for medical practice. A lot of books are moved into circulation. Marketing is marketing.

Ric had also made a distasteful (racist) reference on his website about a Chinese physician, which pissed me off and I called him on it. That also did not go over very big. Nevertheless, the day before his surgery, he still came over to our town, and we still went for one of our walks, this time with me pushing his wheelchair-like contraption, and he making the navigational decisions. I had sent him the following e-mail just before our hike:

> "All I know of love
> is that love is all there is."
>
> Emily was the poet, Lorna is the giver,
> the words face me every day.
>
> I do not argue. But, like Mary,
> I "ponder these things in my heart:"
> if "love is all there is" –
> where does the other stuff come from?
>
> Congenitally, I'm a theologian.
> While you have an audience.
> I now simply play a computer.
>
> Wisdom is different. But whatever –
> we two Old Guys are on a roll.
> I feel better, more relaxed,
> less worried, confident, after this
> writing reading writing reading

dance we just did – do – and are.

Days ago,
while committed to hitting the "send" button,
I already regretted, "racist,"
but the finger had descended.
As you responded –
well, it just goes to show.

I loved a *New Yorker* article on the days
  of Manhattan's Mayor Fiorello LaGuardia
(the "little flower").
At some politico meeting,
a councilman said, while
LaGuardia was ranting,
"Would someone hit that little wop
  in the head."
Oh for my youth with a little politically
  incorrect language.

In any event, celebrate clarity,
piss on pain,
wander with whales.

We're in touch.
Talking we always can do,
but what I am looking forward to
is walking again with you.

Seeing Ric at the hospital, two days after his surgery,
mobile beyond any expected ordinary hospital recovery practice, was quite an experience.

This man is a willing life-force. Ego, shmee-go, selling,
or singing, this guy gets the job of living done under
conditions theologically known as "the conditions of
existence."

Ric has a life-skill to live. He does not look away.
The poetry has the candor it has because he is an
honest man.

Make no mistake; the true import of his work is his
living witness that you too can see and speak – and
live.

I have a limitation regarding Ric's poetry. Contrary
to his having to hear my writing in order to read it,
I read his work instead of hearing it.

One of our early arguments was on the merit of
reading poetry (my preference) or hearing it (both
an historic and contemporary practice). In my
defense, there obviously can be a communicative
use of various fonts, spacings in the layout of words,
unpronounceable words (e. g. in reference to g-o-d
stuff) which has to be seen. But, I should also admit
that, for a variety of reasons, I tend to stay far from
the world of performance.

Ric, on the other hand, besides following in the great
tradition from Homer to modern folk-singers, has
performed across the breadth of the U.S., Canada,
and England, before about every age, selection, and
collection of audience you can imagine (Harvard,
Lenny's Pub, the White House, or the graduating
class of some Central High).

13

I once went to one of Ric's public readings. That evening there was an underlying consistency to the audience's continually misplaced laughter and applause. Both acts worked to render superficial what were sensitive human references in his reading. The inner self of most audience members was kept safely distant – at best, covered. Ric was too often made to become cute or maudlin.

Where/when performance rules potentially meaningful discourse, so does applause – or booing. No one likes being booed. I early on wrote Ric, "I am a good correspondent, but a poor audience."

Make no mistake, though!

The written words of Ric's poems (which you are about to see) are worthy of your sight. They are rich with meaning. His language respects the intimate meeting of reader and author which only the privacy and quiet of the act-of-reading can offer.

Ric has never been a part of the dumbing-down of the citizenry; for example, the "campaign to infantilize the American public," which Susan Sonntag wrote took place after 9/11 with those who had voice and responsibility, especially in leadership positions within National Institutions – Government, the Fourth Estate, Churches.

Ric's import, in his books, on his website, and available in his public readings (when the audience will allow a little intimacy – or courage – into their lives)

is his witness to the truth that you, dear reader, are also a person who can see and speak – and live.

> "when Sybil comes/she comes/with doors and windows/and you can see your mountain/ through her eyes/when Sybil comes/she draws aside the curtains/and the lilac and the lupine/take you by surprise"
> – Ric

Ric's been dying for a long time now. Sooner or later he will be successful. We all are. My fantasy of a memorial service for him is quite different from what probably will happen.

I see family, friends, acquaintances, fans, some of those happily-married-by Ric, neighbors, audience members, assembling one morning on the mountain shortly before sunrise. Kennedy steps forward, as the steward of the gathering, and says,

"Good people, last week our troubadour and friend, Ric Masten, died. He gave his crowning performance. Now we are together this early morn. Please sit down. Snuggle up. Settle down. Get near the hearth fires of our hearts.

"Wonderful to see you April, Jeri, Ellen, Billie Barbara, Stuart, all family, Owen, Ron, Warren, May, Reid, Christopher, Bob, Embree, Deborah, Helen, Rosemary – all of us.

"We're going to be quiet with one another for a while,
private with our memory of Ric in our lives,
honoring a relationship which has brought us to this
hilltop. Be comfortable – with body and thought."

After the sun has cleared the horizon ridge,
the colors of its rays stretching across the sky
and out to sea – perhaps touching
a far bank of fog, Kennedy will add,

"Our solar event has happened, as it did yesterday
and will tomorrow. We can count on it.
And Ric is with us – for a long time,
for the rest of our lives;
as dependable as the sun.
Bless us – each and every one of us – in all of our ways.

"Let's go have some coffee and tea with Billie Barbara."

Amongst many gifts, Ric re-christened me with the name,
walker,

formally,
Joaquin Robert

chapter 1

The Personals

Family and Friends

OFFICIAL PORTRAIT

I look so on top of it
brow arched slightly — eyes alive with good humor
jaw set and yet around the mouth the hint of a smile
all of the above below a well-shaped polished dome
but damn — it bothers me to see that face of mine
so full of confidence
gazing out into the not too distant future
which is where I am today
doing my best to recall that place in time

it was taken on request that much I know
and in a studio so I'm sure the thing was posed
clothes carefully chosen — head tipped just so
lips moistened
posture and expression set absolutely right
and yet like a suspicious dollar bill
I hold my glossy image to the light
but still I cannot say if what I see was real or not
but if it was then I fear the hooded photographer
took more than my photograph that day

better to be caught with a finger in my nose
mouth wide open — eyes drooping closed
with a tree that seems to be growing from my ear
appearing like an idiot and yet surrounded
by those who could love me still
if you must take my photograph
wait!... till after the curtain calls are done
and catch me falling off the stage
into the big bass drum

DOWN THE MISSISSIPPI

(Memories of Jubal George Taylor "Puppa"
my grandfather on my mother's side.)

you were over seventy
when you first registered in my pre-school brain
recognized and acknowledged as something more
than an old man leaning on a cane

"Pupa" mother called you — so I did too
wondering why you spent the days
in an overstuffed chair
by a radio that droned endless financial reports
lighting cigars
you sailed through the Depression
on blue chip ships like Texaco

not once do I remember
seeing anyone but family in your house
it was always and only just — Dada and Pupa
Bostonian transplants
describing avocado as tasting like soap
but enjoying them now in California

little boy memories
trickling down from the Junes and Julys
you took up residence in Carmel
summering in the big creaky house on Camino Real

as a teenager every New Year's day
the family went to you
in Pasadena
Maylin Street being but a block
from the course of the Rose Parade
and less than a mile from the football game
you never joined us though
still preferring chair and radio

what struck me most
was that the garage in Pasadena
smelled exactly like the one in Carmel
reminiscent of stale cigar boxes

I was 23 the last time I saw you
you were 92 and adrift on dementia
Dada didn't want me to see you like this
but I insisted

still in that chair — the radio off
a thirteen year old British lad
a newly arrived immigrant
though Americans hardly think of immigrants
as coming from England

the story was
that during your first year in the land of opportunity
you and a friend rafted down the Mississippi
and I believe the tall tale now
because you brought me aboard for a while
describing the shoreline in minute detail
until closing your pale blue eyes
you drifted away on river flow

three months later
I was informed that Puppa
had finally reached the Gulf of Mexico
and looking at it from where I am now
all in all
a rather pleasant way to go

MOTHER LOAD

one of my earliest memories
is that of my mother holding forth
with the story of my birth

"Talk about hard labor!
How about 42 hours' worth...
Doctor Hugh hauling on the forceps
like a frontier dentist.
And pain so intense
I doubt if even the most dedicated
masochist could bare it.
Ricky's silly little elongated head
appearing at last,
all red and resembling a carrot.
Honestly,
when I saw how pointed he was
I went into hysterics.
Guffawing till stitches burst
and had to be re-sewn.
I mean I really thought the nurse
had brought me an ice-cream cone!"

god
how I resented being grist
for mother's sense-of-humor mill
remaining pissed until my own children
made me face the fact
that for all intents and purposes
I have taken the same act on the road

time
to stop mining the mother load
to quit whining and go to her defense
and say on her behalf
that...
"She knew it wasn't funny
but she loved to make you laugh."

A SMALL QUIET WAR

over the years my wife and I
have discovered two things
a man and a woman
should avoid doing together
that is
if they value their relationship
laying rugs
and carrying mattresses

and she's at it again
my wife
under the house digging

I can hear her down there
with my old rusty tools
picking and shoveling away
hollowing out a place
for her imagination to run wild in

she's been at it off and on now
for two years
running back and forth
with one shovelful of dirt at a time
throwing it into the yard
doing it the hard way
and I must admit
I'm always a bit surprised
and annoyed
when I see the size of the pile
she is making
but it's her project and she says
I'm not
and don't have to be involved

still and all
it has now become impossible
for me to lie here comfortably
listening to the ball game

WORDS

Have I told you your smile
It comes without warning
Brings pictures of kitchen
Of honey and morning,
And sunshine
And yellow canary birds sing
But words are just words —
Your smile
Now, that's the real thing

And the sound of your laugh
When we're running together
Like wind in the shingles
And October weather.
Like pushing the children
Up high on a swing
The sound of your laugh
That's the real thing!

Have I told you "I love you.?"
Well, how could I say it
With couplets and verses
I'd never convey it.
Words may be pretty
As beads on a string
But words are just words
Will you settle
For the real thing?

PREMONITION A WEEK BEFORE THE MOTORCYCLE WRECK

Nathan is
but Nathan doesn't know it yet

and so he comes in a cloud of dust
and he has removed the muffler
from his machine
and we can hear him coming
for ten deafening minutes
hair wild
shirt open
a scar on his hard young belly
he steals my wine
rolls cigarettes
and he can spit at least fifteen feet
Nathan can

and even before the dust has settled
he is gone
with my son down the road
shouting and yelling

Nathan
I hope you look down soon
and find your shadow
before you hurt yourself
and/or all of us

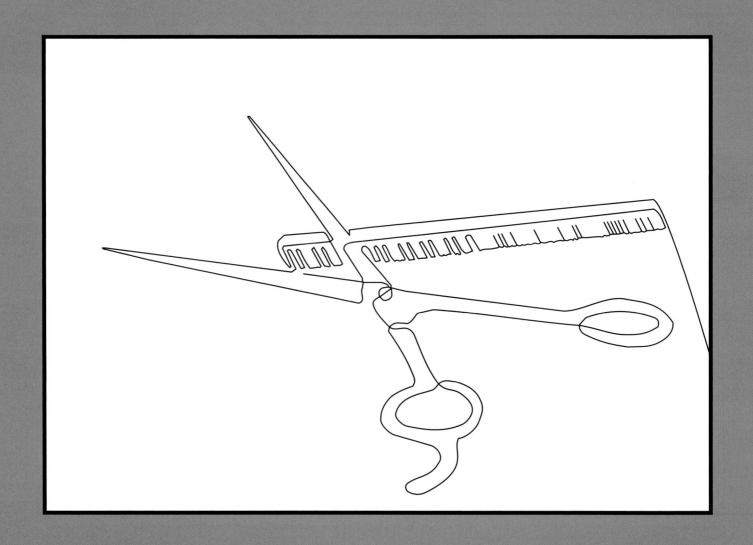

Genesis House

in the driveway of a renovated apartment complex dwarfing a chair
the continent of Africa sat getting a haircut
the barber — a Latina wore soiled institutional whites
I slowed to first gear. "I'm looking for Genesis House", I said
and the haircut said: "You're here. Visitors register over there."

I followed the motion of his head to a doorway marked "Office"
a group of marginal looking people stood around it chain smoking
eyeing me suspiciously — one of them approached
"Hi Dad, I didn't think anyone would come." and why should he
considering all the years of lies manipulation and denial
"Neither did I." I said signing in

after that it was a minefield — father and son taking up positions
at opposite ends of the dusty old couch that sat outside in the courtyard
gingerly stepping around the dangerous ground
avoiding the obvious trip wires — sticking to safe subjects
I held my tongue determined not to set him off or blow up myself
perhaps later in the recovery we can sweep the relationship clean
digging up and disarming the booby traps
but for now to survive the war for even a short visit
would be more than enough

getting up to go I told him about how much we enjoyed taking care
of his son Little Ricky and about waiting at the mailboxes each day
to meet the car pool sadly adding the grim footnote that when he was a boy
coming home from school I can't remember ever doing as much for him
"Well you did today, Dad."
as I left I looked back and was surprised to see the haircut
and some of the other residents waving.....as if I were family

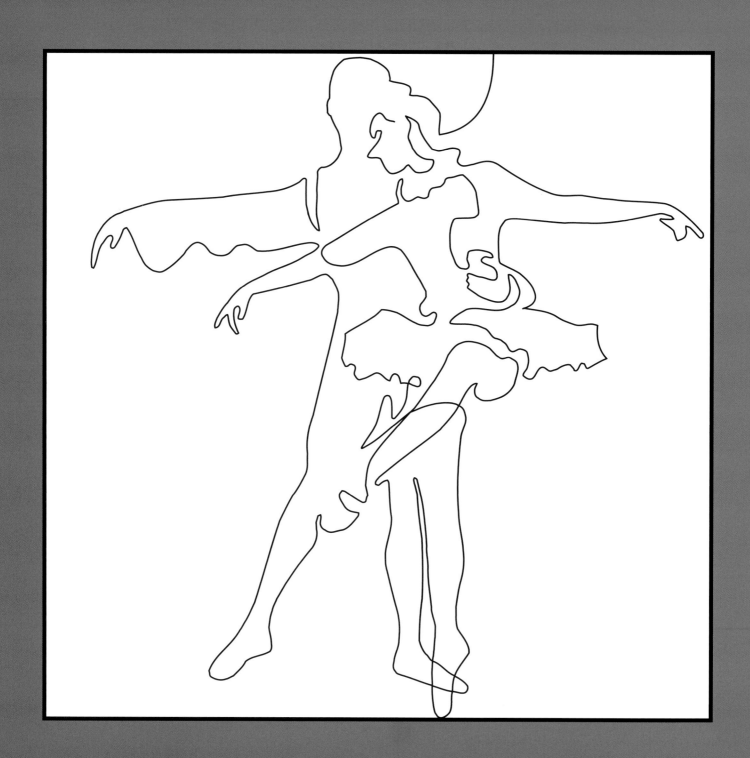

ELLEN

my youngest daughter
likes to ride to the mailbox with me
she fetches the mail
while I turn the car around
then, climbs into the back seat
and doles out my letters slowly
inspecting each envelope
'till I am infuriated
turned red and shout
"Ellen, give me the letters!"
my youngest daughter liked to do this!
it is one of the few times
she has my full attention

during these annoying episodes
her negative demeanor
brought to mind the ugly duckling
not that Ellen was the least bit unattractive
but her contrary stubborn nature
drove us all up the wall
the family deciding on a movie,
which Ellen refused to see
a walk on the beach? — "I'll get sand in my eye."
flying kites? — "Too cold and windy."

later she gravitated
to teaching English as a second language
which meant that for years
all the eager young swains she brought home
didn't speak a word of English
which much to Ellen's delight
left her type A extrovert father
gesturing dumbly at wall and ceiling
mumbling "Mi casa. Ha Ha Ha."

and of course it follows
that she would be captured and carried off
by one of these foreign invaders
an over-bearing Spanish artist

who at the time
was painting a penis six feet high
"Es expresion politica!" says he
"self portrait," thought I

but good comes out of bad
our granddaughter Gaia, the rarest of pearls
produced by this agitated oyster
which in time would be terminated
by bottles of wine and verbal abuse

we beseeched Ellen to come home
and settle here in the West
but once again contrary to our hopes and wishes
she took a job on the East Coast
in a private school directing the ESL program

given enough time however
things do become transformed
ducklings not withstanding
Ellen coming to visit accompanied
by a very handsome tall articulate fellow
English speaking! I might add
announcing
that they were engaged to be married
and sure enough
the following summer they did return
to have me minister the grand affair

this time around
Ellen came down the aisle
dressed in white
doing it all exactly right
every trace of contrary duckling gone
dancing with her Baryshnikov
my youngest daughter
the swan

JERRALDINE

dutiful daughter — first-born child
plugging in the coffee pot while I punch
the dial
trying to locate your foolhardy baby sister
lost in the bowels of Mexico City
last seen with someone called "Paco"...
next to this coffee gets cold

at Christmas the traditional
beautifully wrapped knit cardigan
almost missed this year — stacked up
against
your brother's six-month chip
my gratitude skimmed off
by his clean and sober reappearance
I track this miracle one day at a time
the sweaters piling up — fraying at the
wrist

what happens to the siblings of prodigals
is the epitome of irony and so before your
father
becomes too senile
to distinguish between stranger and kin
with tears welling in my eyes
I recognize you now
and thank you for being there when
to wipe the drool off an old fool's chin

APRIL AT LONG LAST

April — born the last day of
April almost Mae...
And I have enjoyed the word play
your mother never suspecting that an April
once had this love sick boy lying on my tummy
with the Sunday funnies whispering her name
as I followed her exploits in
Terry and the Pirates from frame
to electrifying frame

so now you know
where the April came from
but what about you, daughter number two?
playing with the language the way
baby Mozart played piano from his crib
at three so adorably glib
"Dad, 'maybe' is just a slow 'No'"
or surprised by the horizon
"Hey, I've got my far eyes on"
"Aprilizms" plagiarized
swiped from your erudite bib and embedded
in my verse without giving credit

even worse
it has recently been brought to my attention
that you have been neglected
ignored completely in your father's work
true — I only write
when the pain and puzzlement
demand a formal "think"
and certainly up to now your younger siblings
soaked up all that ink
reams of rhyme in which you are scarcely a ghost
"Don't feel guilty, Pop, "I've always known
 that you love me the most."

which in itself creates a quandary
I do play favorites
but isn't the heart compartmentalized enough
to have a special place for all of you?
over time I find the most preferred
is the one that crisis has put in my sights
the offspring upon who the focus
of my fatherly concern is forced to light

so April, at long last
this one's for you

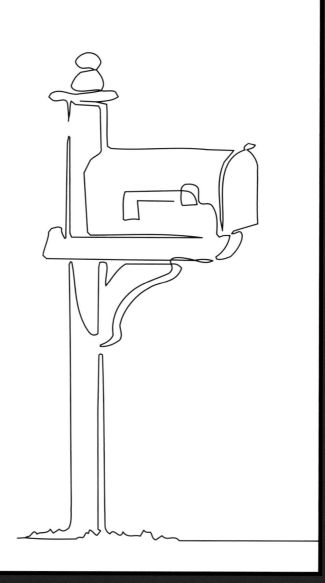

PARENTS

unopened as yet
the envelope
turns in my hand
and I suppose
the Flying Wallendas can
but I never could
stand at ease
watching my children
play in the woods
play in the trees
so certain was I
that they would fall
and they did
and they didn't

but now
that they have grown
old as I was then
out on their own
sending messages home
as to where they are
and how they have been
the envelope
turns in my hand
and nothing
has changed at all

GRANDPA

PHOENIX

after he completed basic training
my grandson...
my namesake calls
       "I have some good news Grandpa."
       "What?" I ask cautiously
       "I got a tattoo!"
       "You what? Where?" I shouted
       "On my right deltoid."
       "How big is it?"
       "About six inches tall."
       "Oh, Ric, you damn fool. What is it?"
       "It's the Phoenix. You know, rising up
        out of the ashes. It's cool."
       "Is there a name involved?"
       "Yep."
       "Some floozy I suppose."
       " No. The bird is rising out of the word
       'Grandpa' — like me out of you."
       "Awww," says I beginning to bawl
"That is one smart kid!"
  remarked my son-in-law

I should have known though
that good news comes with bad
and sad to say
the Phoenix has flown to Iraq
my namesake doing a tour of duty
in that deadly situation
where there is a target tattooed
on every GI's back

I drive a car which I'm told
makes me part of this power play
this irrational conflict
this war that isn't quite a war
but more a national deltoid display
our fledglings put in harm's way
and for the life of me
I can't say why or what for

last night I dreamed I saw the Phoenix
rising from this conflagration
up up to vanish in the high vaulted blue
down below ashes scattering
disturbed as the nightmare gallops through

PONY ISLAND

submerged in sadness
I acknowledge the relentless
passage of time
Pony Island is gone
and oddly the demolition was done by me
I say oddly
because from the nineteenth of July
to the twelfth of August
I watched entranced
while my visiting granddaughters
worked the fantasy out in the dirt driveway
below my writing-room window

Cara
the solemn nine-year-old bossing the job
with Gaia — a lively firecracker five
taken on as the tireless "go fer"
the two of them spending
the long summer afternoons
raiding the wood box
pilfering rocks from the garden walls
sneaking my tools out of the shop
digging and scraping
shaping the pliable surface
into every little girl's
enchanted sandbox dream

barn and stables
paddock and polo field
a steeplechase — a race track
pastures — pond and stream
all of this surrounded by bright blue water
an equestrian Bali Ha'i
set in the center of a make-believe sea
"Pony Island!" Cara proclaimed as Gaia
meticulously — breathlessly — endlessly
explained the intricate topography

but as previously revealed
this enchanted domain is no more
because for reasons I have yet to understand
the moment I returned home from the airport
I went with shovel and rake in hand
directly to the now abandoned building site
and almost without thinking
strangely driven — a man possessed
I thoroughly policed the area
returning blocks and sticks
to the wood box
filling in ditches furrows and holes
removing
the carefully placed rocks and twigs
raking and watering
until there was nothing left — nothing

except the awful melancholy inside
at the center— like an island
and the sound of hoof beats racing off
down a deserted beach
disappearing the way time does

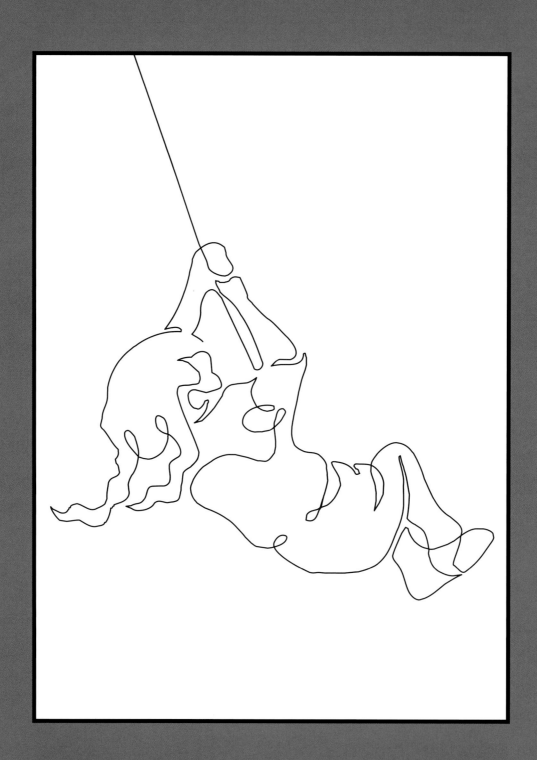

PEBBLES & CRUMBS

last summer
whenever possible
my visiting granddaughter Cara
would worm
her tiny hand into mine
and like Hansel and Gretel
we'd strike out from the house
up the "barking dog trail"
to the "creaky swings"
don't you love the labels
little children put on things?
and after a few "sky flying"
"watch me, Grandpa"
it was on to the "sneaky table"
where hidden in the shade
beneath a giant live oak tree
we would split
the forbidden can of Coke I brought
— damn it, Dad, her teeth will rot!

rested and refreshed
we then ascend
the "slidey steep"
to check the water level
in the "water keep"
to lift the lid and take a peek
then down the trail
in single file we go
through the "witchy woods"
all the way to Arizona
which is what my spouse
has dubbed the shack
she uses as her dream shop
and studio
Grandma, it seems, also
has a knack for naming things
"— if anyone calls
            tell them I'm in Arizona"

next stop —
the family memorial garden
where we solemnly commune
with the trees
Kim and Emil have become
chanting softly as we pass
— from ashes to ashes
            to flowering plum

then wending our way
along a stretch of "dusty dirt"
we search for yesterday's
footprints
covering them with today's
"backward walking" sometimes
— to fool our enemies
            and friends

and always
during the final leg
of this backyard expedition
my companion lags behind
little Miss Slowpoke
gathering specimens —
repeating after me the name
of every trailside
shrub and tree
eucalyptus   sticky monkey
lilac   sage   madrone
and don't touch that
it's poison oak
then suddenly
"—We're home!"

last summer
Cara and I collected
and polished these moments
leaving them along the path
like pebbles
to be used
in the distant future
the way
a whiff of cigar smoke
brings my grandfather back
to poke about in the garden
with his walking stick
the way
my grandmother's face
magically appears
at the taste of peppermint
her watchful presence
close at hand
whenever I shake sand
from something
that has been to the beach

I know that on some
faraway tomorrow
a sip of Cola on a hot day —
a pinch of sage —
the creaking sound
a rope swing makes
these things with Cara's help
can bring me back
to life again
and thankful as I am
for such life-extending crumbs
sadly I also know
that the cigar smoke
and peppermint trick
can only be done by me —
in a couple of generations
it all becomes
a banquet for the crows

chapter 2

I Should Have Slept On It

Writing & Performing

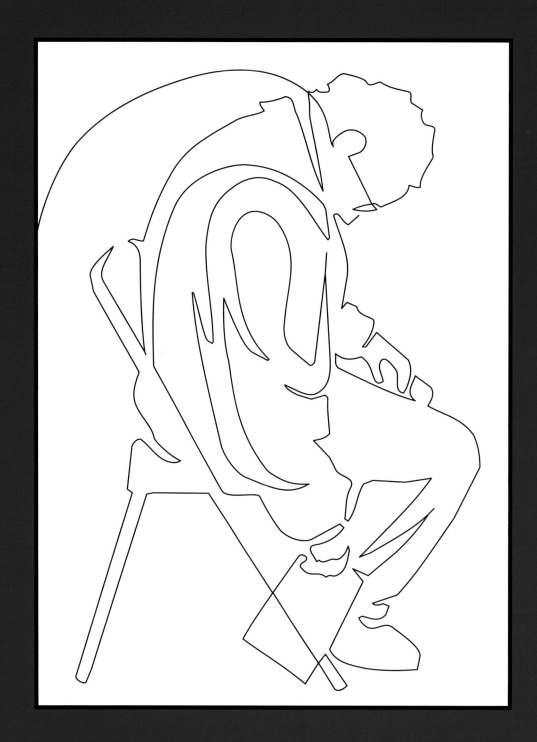

A SLEEPER

to be a poet reading
is chancy work at best
tough enough to face rejection
but worse
far worse — this

you fell asleep
even as I read you closed your eyes
and dropped
your head upon your chest
and to this day
I marvel that you kept your seat
nodding east
and west

and although I find it sad
I guess it's only human
that looking back upon a sea
of open faces
I can best recall the one that slept
and wonder
were you overtired
or simply bored
with all that I expressed

only now writing this
years later
have I thought to ask about the dream
you might have had that day
and all
I may have missed

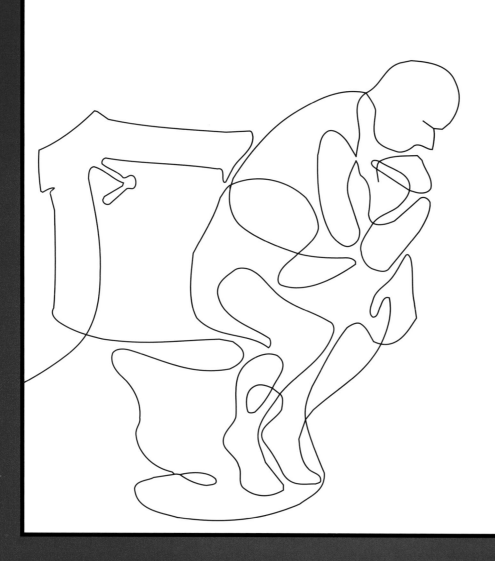

FACING A DEADLINE WITH WRITER'S CRAMP

"I want that poem on my desk
by 2:30 Friday afternoon!"
this
when nothing rhymes with 'orange'
and I find myself caught
in a period of poetic irregularity

each day like a good boy
I sit down at a prescribed time to do my duty
and that's it
I just sit trying to force a line
stuck behind locked doors
bearing down for hours and nothing moving
except the patterns in the tile
where I stare at the floor

what's a body to do
when the rhymes don't come through?
there must be something a poet
could be privy to
some trick of nature like prunes or castor oil

I've been told that a sudden calamity can be
cathartic
that you can have the verses scared out of you
I know that a friend and a bottle of wine
can loosen things up
but believe me it's no fun
facing a deadline
knowing ya got one in there
but ya can't get it out

maybe I'm pregnant
maybe having a poem is like having a baby
they come when they're ready
little creatures howling into our lives
with a mind of their own

in any event
it's not happening here
and I've reached the point in this one
where it is obvious
I need either a mild laxative
or a natural disaster

THIS I WOULD SAY TO GRADUATES

imagine a high school all-school-required assembly
students being herded in a cell block at a time
looking for reasons to riot –
the principal stands glaring on the apron of the stage
staring the restless mob down into an unstable quiet
now imagine a poet being introduced to this

I learned early on
not to begin my remarks going for a laugh
encouraging some young clown out there in the dark
to bark Ha! Ha! Ha! -- no, I just tell them the truth
that I have "terminal" cancer
that for eleven years my son was a crack addict
that for me poetry is trying to put a line of language
around the pain and puzzlement – corralling them
to better comprehend that which is troubling me
I don't write about things I understand
I write to better understand about things

then, and this is most important, I tell the students
that rather than be stuck with me, a poet,
for the next fifty minutes "Go in your mind
to that activity and place where you would rather be."
after a pause I say, "Now ask yourself
if you could earn a living doing that --- there?"

always laughter to which I respond
"Well, I suppose you could make your livelihood
as a test dummy in a mattress factory
or clean the windows of the Playboy Mansion
but seriously if the answer is "no" then are you doomed
to spend the rest of your life as alienated labor

what would you say the odds are
against a person being able to make a good living
composing and performing poetry in America?
a billion-to-one I bet and yet you can't see me
as the flower from a nonexistent plant

I would wish that every graduate would leave
the ivied halls of academia
with their dream intact
convinced that anything is possible

*(Written for and delivered at the Eighth Annual
Celebration of Community on April 27, 2005,
when Ric Masten was honored by being named
the "Distinguished Fellow in the Arts"
by California State University, Monterey Bay.)*

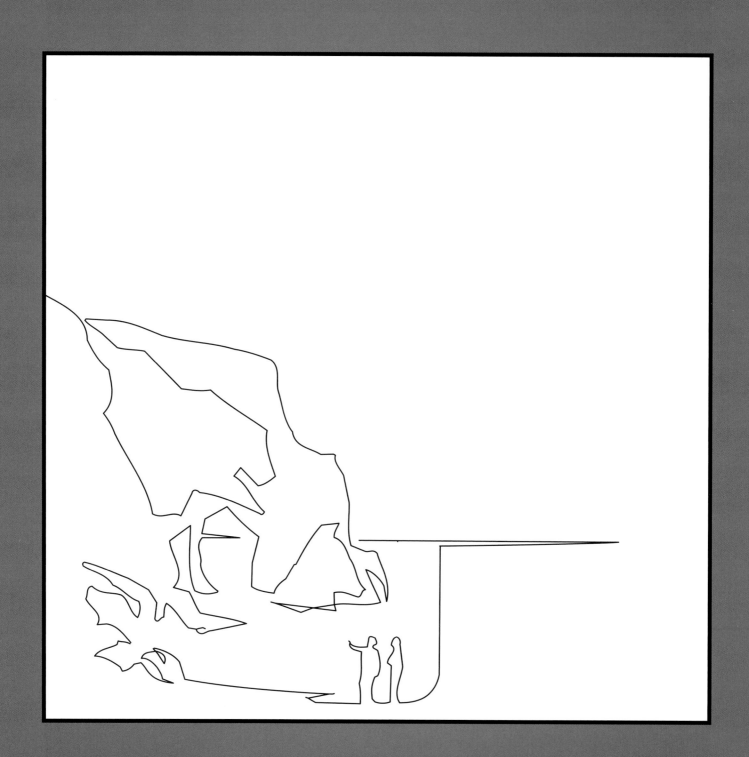

THE CHALLENGE

(For Francisco X. Alarcón,
a poet of enormous talent and girth,
brimming
with mesoamerican wisdom —
Latin American mirth.

And for Javier,
a delightfully shy young man
with limited English
but a handsome piñata
full of sweet surprises.)

the Pacific
was particularly playful that day
racing back and forth
tickling our feet
sneaking up behind to splash us
in the seat of the pants
then dancing away
giggling

at the base of the cliff
where the sand ends
there is a natural granite bridge
if you stand at just the right place
the horizon winks at you
through the opening

"What shall we call it?"
Francisco challenges
"I will call it: ¡La Puerta al Mar!
The Doorway to the Sea!"
the 1993
National Book Award winner
dares me to be as creative

what a pregnant occasion!
what a rare opportunity
to raise
the level of my poetic stock
but phrases like "Punctured Stone"
and "Neptune's Peephole" elude me
after a long ponderous minute
all I can think of is:
"¡Rock with a Hole in it!"

a week later
retracing our footprints
I still wallow
in the waves of laughter

OLD ROBERT FROST

I saw old Robert Frost
in Pasadena last Fall
he stumbled around
in a celluloid dream
that somebody caught and kept
old Robert Frost
stirring his milk with a spoon
till it spilled
and I said to myself
"Why you old crafty buffoon."

in one of his lighter moments
he remarked with a wink
that you can't write a poem
to pay a bill
"That's not what they're for."

so I think I'll extend
that thought
this much more
having nothing else in the bank
no savings at all
except old Robert Frost
and a wolf at the door

I SHOULD HAVE SLEPT ON IT

being published
means something only
on the date of publication
had I known this
I would never have listed
my occupation as "Poet"
when filling out
and filing my income tax forms

I would have been better off
had I described myself as "Voyeur"
or "Manic-depressive"

I can see now
I should have slept on it
accomplishments never seem to survive
a good night's sleep

the rejection slips however...
the dead ends
are always there in the morning
like that bully-kid
who gave me such a hard time
on the way to school

sneering
asking me again today
"And what it is
that you really do for a living?"

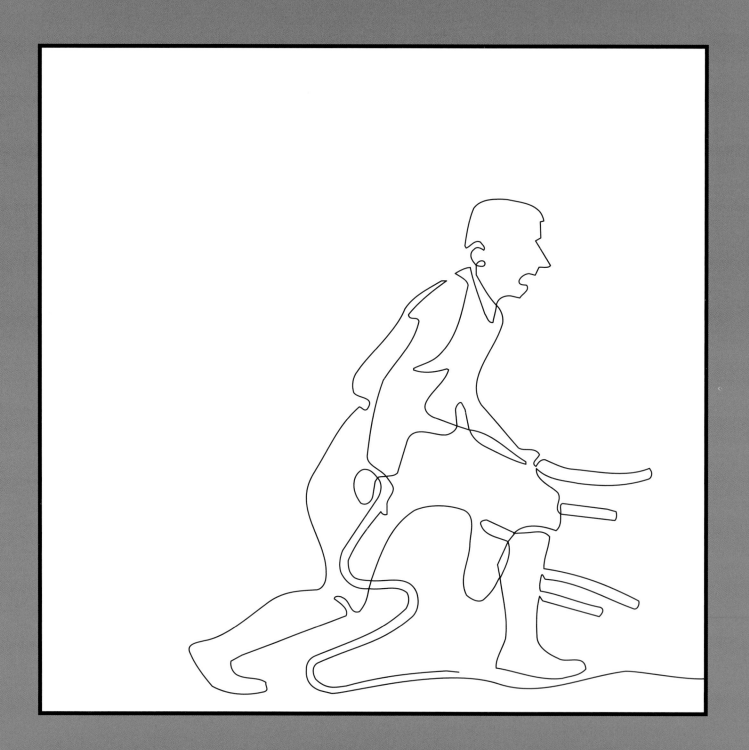

THE LION TAMER ENTERS THE THESAURUS
AND ESCAPES WITH HIS LIFE

I don't like to write!

words are nasty
uncooperative animals
stubborn unruly beasts
and I despise every minute
I put in with whip and chair
attempting to make them behave

sure, I take a bow
when I have them all lined up
in an impressive row
my vulnerable ego
having somehow escaped
critical analysis without
being clawed or bitten
but I don't like to write

I like having written

PLIGHT OF THE SERIOUS WRITER

I once complained
to an astute and insightful
writer friend
about being bogged down
in a torturously long
and nonproductive dry spell

gravely
he considered my sad situation
then with great compassion
and empathy
said:

"So, life
 is treating you that well,
 is it?"

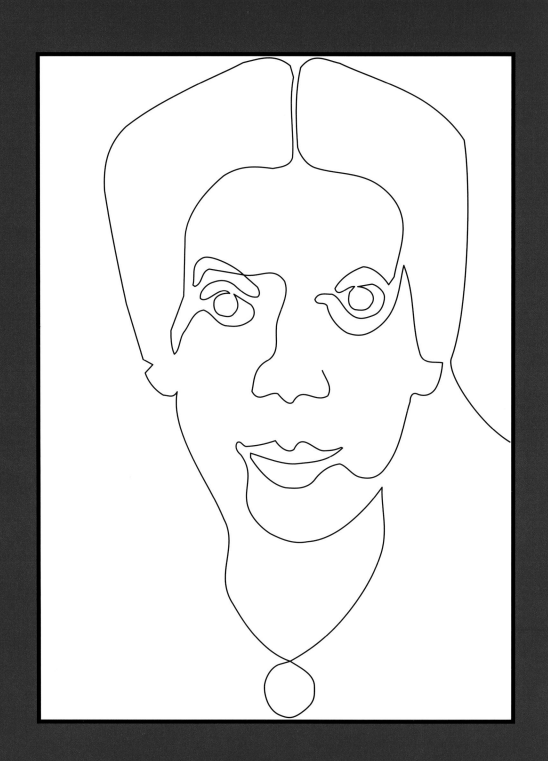

CLOSET POETS

I suspect you know precisely
how many poems fit in a cardboard box
perhaps even
the number of boxes it takes
before the furniture must go

who are you keeping
the secrets for, though?
yourself?
and/or that vague romantic notion
you have
of being found up in the attic
some future kindred spirit
sitting on a dusty trunk
weeping over your mildewed remains

Emily Dickinson
was already at the cemetery
when Colonel Tom Higginson
went to the closet
and discovered
her collection of damask...
hand-sewn dreams
neatly folded away like fine linen

lucky for us
he and her inheritors
were a determined
self-serving enterprising bunch

certainly everyone
admires a shy private person
but be advised
without the pump of ambition
all the talent in the world
can come to no more
than a couple of trips to the dump

GARDEN PAVILION

yesterday
I would have told you that depression
was simply the "downer" that follows
rejection or setback
a shallow moody dimple
difficult but manageable
bleak doldrums that usually respond
to: "Come on now! Snap out of it!"

at worst
depression would be a debilitating low
a slow turning whirlpool in which
one becomes trapped in the undertow
treading water
sapped of all enthusiasm
caught in a murky atmosphere
where darkness and apathy rule

not so! — not so!
depression turns out to be
more like a violent brain storm
the cranium an electric arena
of unrelenting action
blackness charged with angst
unbridled thoughts stampeding
death — ill-health — poverty
like psychedelic film clips the subject matter
suddenly turns suicidal
and I see myself involved
with Skil-saws — carbon monoxide
X-acto knives — second story swan dives

hypnotic — demonic
psychotic suggestions taking aim
until at wits end my family
deposits me in the Garden Pavilion
an elegant name for the local loony bin

I awake to walls and ceilings —
very very white with nary
a dark corner anywhere in sight
halls crawling with counselors and shrinks
the posted daily schedule clogged
with therapies and group activities
enough
to give our disturbed minds no time to think
three days it took to break the fall
to turn around and begin the long haul out
climbing up the line
"better living through chemistry"

back on firmer ground I visit
my own poetic archives
to see what I had to say yesterday
about those who gave in
to depression and suicide

and I find I have apologies to make
to David "unwilling to face another day"
to Ann Sexton
for "going down beneath the hooves!"
to Sylvia Plath who traded her bell jar
for a hissing gas stove
to Stevie Smith and John Berryman
"waving — even as they fell"
and to Vincent Van Gogh for falling prey
to "his blinding field of hay."

to all of you that I have criticized
for taking the final step
surveying it
from recent lived experience
my arrogant proclamations
seem totally inept

knowing what I now know
it's time to go back to the punch lines
and soften the blow

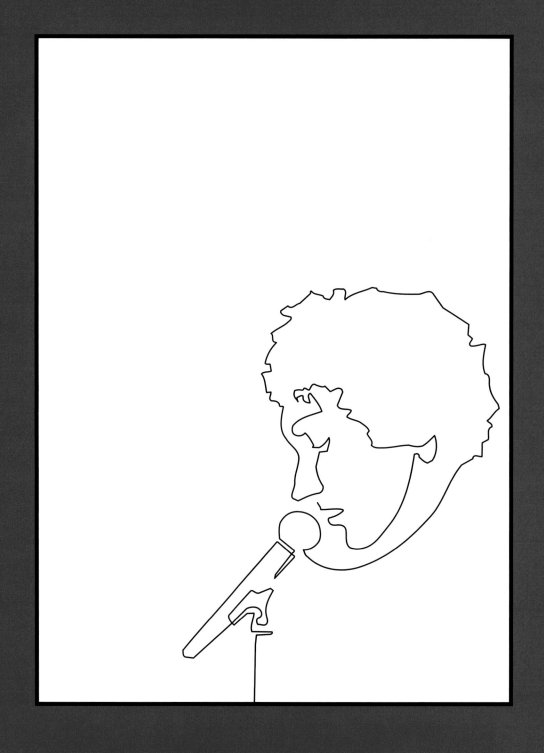

LIKE THE SPARROW

for Brendan Constantine

it was 1948 in the City of Lights
fresh from the States I was an easy target
for the money changers haunting the alleyways
around the American Embassy — the new beret,
wide-pile corduroys and squeaky shoes fooled no one
"Hey, Yank, you got money to change?"

in that first week I went to hear
the "Little Sparrow" sing
Edith Piaf, the reigning diva of the time
appearing on stage to deafening applause
bowing, blowing kisses until quiet ruled
she began weaving her spell with La Vie En Rose
breaking my heart as the number ended
her voice trailing off into melancholy

"Bravo!" I came to my feet clapping my hands the
silent audience staring me back down into my seat
I got it then — one number heralding the next
an uninterrupted kaleidoscope of song
and when at last she finished her set
the audience rose
and we gave her a fifteen minute ovation

this old memory surfaced the evening I went sailing
with you, Brendan—two featured poets at Tebot Bach
you launched first but the choppy water
stirred up by sudden squalls of laughter
bursts of applause got in my way
of course I saw the cleverness and humor
but had no idea how deep the water was

parting we bartered books
and while driving back to Sur
the love of my life read your words aloud
and I was thrilled
by the journey you had carefully charted
one poem leading into another
the surface calm enough now
to fathom the depth of you — the deep purple blue
I had missed the night before

without the spray and foam of frenetic fans
I could hear you and it was as if the sparrow
sang us all the way home

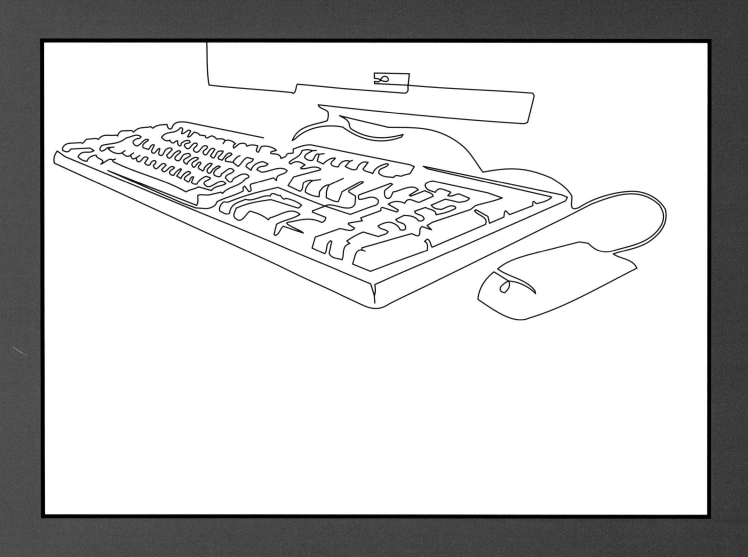

I was having an earnest discussion about "why people write" with my friend Joaquin Robert, when he suddenly opens his wallet and lovingly brings out this little yellowed newspaper clipping, saying in a hushed voice: "To write, is to write, is to write." He then read me the much-fingered fragment of a larger piece by Charles Mcabe, a columnist for the San Francisco Chronicle.

"By writers I mean people who have something to say and have to say it. They do not always say it brilliantly, and often their efforts are not published at all. There is an obsessional quality in this kind of writing. It is an obsession for which we should all be grateful – that a man or woman gives us their felt experience with little thought of the reward. Most write for 'financial reward,' or, 'for a public or for publishers or for both.'"

Concluding, Joaquin eyes me sideways, knowingly -- but I haven't got a clue as to what my friend is trying to tell me. And "no clue," as always equals "my cue." Time to build a word corral. Time to try and get a line of language around the puzzlement. And if successful, I'll close the gate and we can look inside to see if I have captured something new.

LIKE BREATHING?

I simply don't understand
you say: to write is to write is to write
a puzzling circular statement
that smacks of roses
do you mean like breathing?
if you don't do it — you die
breathing
being automatic but also something
that can be controlled and directed

me?
I am my writing — no more, no less
in the beginning was the word
but I wasn't —
not until I began to type myself out
write myself down and if I,
with this written identity,
don't greet you with a poem
you don't interest me — when we part
if I haven't given you my book
we never connected

do I write for the money?
that's funny — what money?
recognition, applause, even acid criticism
are human interactions
interplay tells me where I am
and that you are aware of my presence

and really, I don't like to write
no more than I enjoy changing
I'm stubborn and will always tell you
I'm content to be where I am
but after a forced transition
painful as it may have been
I'm always excited
with the "who" I have just written
and can't wait to recite myself for you

to write is to write is to write
your chest rising and falling
in concert with keyboard sound
while over here
I have just jotted myself down

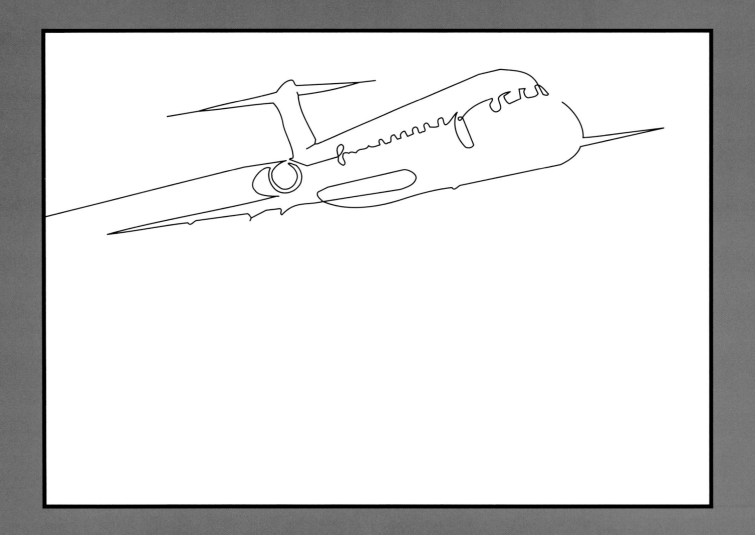

THINK OF ME AS MUSIC

Wake me in the morning,
Take me to the plane.
Yesterday is over now,
Tomorrow never came.
It's time to get the guitar down
And hit the friendly skies.
Time to have another 'round
Of helloes and good-byes.

Well, I guess I let my coffee
Sit there getting cold.
I really didn't want it though,
Just something warm to hold,
While I look at you and wonder
Why a good thing has to end
And if I'll ever pass this way
And be with you again.

Gonna taxi down that runway,
Turn around to go
And as we climb and circle
I'll look for you below.
And somewhere in the future
Alone with my guitar
I'll sing for you...
This song for you...
And you know who you are.

So think of me as music.
Think of me as rhyme.
And if you ever need a friend
Just bring me to your mind.
But like a melody,
I've just got to be
Free to drift along,
So I think I'm gonna
Change my name
And call myself a song.

In forty-seven minutes
They'll put that big bird down.
I'll step into an airport...
Play another town.
Meet another stranger...
Make another friend.
Share a song...
Get it on...
And then be gone again.

So think of me as music.
Think of me as rhyme.
And if you ever need some love
Just bring me to your mind.
But like a melody,
I've just got to be
Free to sail along.
So I think I'm gonna
Change my name
And call myself a song.

chapter 3

Reading the Road Signs

Social Action

THE FAN

you ask:
do I know Joan Baez?
Well, let me count the ways

it was the Summer of '67
in the afterglow
of a Big Sur celebration
she was barefoot
and wore a blue velvet gown
her presence filled the room
and children followed
her around

we had a friend in common
who brought us together
laughing as we joggled
cups and saucers
from one hand to the other
her touch was firm and cool
and though
a hundred years go by
I'll not forget
what Joanie had to say
the day
we held each other
in each other's eye

"Hi."

or are you really asking:
does Joan Baez know
that she knows me?

VANISHING SPECIES

I was born on a planet
almost seventy light years from here

an idyllic world
where children grew up
without the threat of nuclear holocaust
or ecological strangulation
no instant systems of communication
no black revolutions
gay revolutions
drug revolutions
no women's liberation
not even the choice
of taking or not taking the pill
an Eden really

true
the seed of all this was there
but had nothing to do
with my formative years

and now
I find myself come to this harsh place
a kind of space traveller
having close encounters
with my own children

like creatures
from different star systems
we stare at each other
across the void
even our words have different stems

we are aliens in each other's midst

but damn it
I am the one saddled with the memory
of that other place
part of a colony
stranded on planet earth
at the end of the twentieth century
marooned
with no way to go back
and no time to go on

like a moon being eclipsed
my kind will soon be gone
and in light of the headlines today
the sooner the better

READING THE ROAD SIGNS

gridlocked —
gripping the steering wheel
inching forward in fits and starts
I wonder about the trouble ahead....
a well-known pessimist once said
that like a snowball
rolling toward the lip of a ledge
America's problems have grown
so enormous
that what little we could do
to change direction
would simply not be enough
to keep us from going over the edge

I'd like to say I don't agree
but stalled here on the freeway
I see opportunist after opportunist
pull out and speed away
using the shoulder illegally
the law-breakers
too numerous now to be arrested
they know the CHP
will only merge them back in
near the head of the line
a thousand cars better off than before
and seeing this I realize
that these are the kind of people
who succeed in business

yesssss!
you can almost hear them hiss
pumping a fist
slapping the dash in victory
back up to speed
we head for the crash

A PLACE FOR CONSERVATIVES

I must admit it bothers me more
than just a little bit
to see an airline pilot with dandruff
sitting around slightly wrinkled
chewing gum looking like any one of us
I mean, when you see the crew
go passing through the gate
don't you want the captain to be
a tight-lipped man
with close-cropped hair
eyes like steel doors slammed shut
crisp white shirt
slacks creased so sharply
if you weren't careful
you could get a nasty cut there

why I'd turn in my boarding pass
just like that
if some freaky long-haired cat
came bopping by
with a nose ring in a nostril
saying "hey baby
I'm gonna take us for a ride"

believe me I'm finally convinced
there really is a place for conservatives
or would you go to a neurosurgeon
who bit his fingernails?
seen knocking his drink over all the time
I mean
would you really want to do business
with either one of these guys
the morning after
he fought all night with his wife?
not on your life – not me at least
if I'm getting on that plane
going under that knife

what we need here
are hard-minded cold-blooded
machine-like people
in a culture as techno-
logically advanced as ours has become
we cannot all afford to be
human

TAP ROOTS

club in hand
back there in the half-light
before the dawn looking out
from under a shelf-like brow
I would watch her with the child
with the life
SHE had created

now this was before the word
and because I knew not the why
nor the how of it
I was filled with envy and rage
and I hated her
for try as I might – strain as I would
I the male could create nothing
more impressive than a turd

wasn't I bigger than her?
and stronger?
so to cover my chagrin and disgrace
I gave her a cuff across the face
took up a stone knife
and walked out into the morning

be patient with me, woman
I'm working on it
but when the tap root
goes down that deep into history
the tree is not easily moved

and now
that you do have your sperm bank
and have mastered karate
have I suddenly
become irrelevant again?

HE BEING HEFTY AND SHE FULL-FIGURED

Don Rickles' sense of humor
would seem mean and vicious
coming out of Robert Redford
so I hope I'm fat and flabby enough
to get away with telling you
about what came to mind
during the tender performance of a love song
composed and rendered by a fat man
for his even fatter fiancée

a seaside song
two silhouettes walking the silver strand
hand-in-hand type song
wind-swept with salty kisses and ocean spray
a beautiful day in a love-life song
but when you know
you're not supposed to think about whales
whales are all you can think about

beached whales frolicking in the surf
the scene in *From Here To Eternity*
played out on an immense corpulent scale
tons of fun heaped on a wet slippery rock
collapsing the dock
acres and acres of sunburn
and footprints two-feet deep

caught in the undertow
swept along on a rip-tide of uncontrollable thought
I almost miss what is most important here
set to music — in song
all of us appear ageless attractive and trim
able to see each other as he saw her
and she saw him

WORDS ARE WEIRD AND HUMANS...?

Sometimes the English language will abandon you completely. Like have you ever gone looking for the word you would use to describe what it was you had left if you happened to lose one of your galoshes? What is that other rubber thing? Goulash being Hungarian stew.

And I've got a "new" for you. "New" being the singular of "news" which is that words are weird, and the weirdest words of all are the obscenities. Like, who invented these? Where did they come from? Did the English-speaking part of the world once hold a great convention? The chair calling the restless throng to order, explaining that some ding-dong would soon invent the automobile. A thing that would be forever breaking down.... Running out of gas and catching our fingers in slamming doors. "Aghhhhh!"

And for sanity's sake at least, we should set aside some forbidden words to use at painful times such as these to help let the steam out. And rising to the occasion, a man of vision shouts "Mr. Chairperson!" (I'm for de-genderization, but what do we do with words like: manhole?) "I suggest that in the English speaking part of the world we use bodily functions as our obscenities."

The motion was seconded and carried unanimously. The jubilant congregation staging a wild twenty-minute demonstration before settling down to the difficult task of hammering out the details. Taking the most intimate human bodily function and making it the most obscene. Then completing the list, heavy on body parts and toilet procedure. Clearly it was one of humankind's finest hours.

And it simply had to be this way, because in other cultures, what we consider obscene and insulting, means no more to them than as if we called a person: A big eye! A little ear! Son of a forehead! In the Orient, however, try calling a person: A pig! Or a dog and see what happens to you. I would guess that at their great gathering a dignified old gentleman rose to propose: "That here in the East, to call a human by an animal name would be the most degrading of insults," and of course, for this wisdom and insight, he was given a standing but polite: Ahhh so!

And so it goes until every radio talk-show host keeps a finger on the panic button: beep beeping out expletives that have become so commonplace and innocuous, even sweet old ladies are overheard at tea-time saying: "Margaret, would you prefer one of two "beeping" lumps?"
And why? Everyone knows what goes on behind the beeps. It must have been that Congress and the media realizes how overworked and useless our curse words have become, and is now breaking ground for the day that when we stub our toe we can go hopping around like the Road Runner "beep beeping."

Perhaps now is the time for another great obscenity assembly. Time to outline this new dilemma and once again throw the floor open for suggestions so that the ever-present man of brilliance can once again propose to thunderous applause: "Mr. Chairperson, the old words have now become so impotent and ineffective that I suggest we change and make the word "nose" the filthiest dirtiest word in the English language." After which, I suppose we would all step into the street going: "Nose man! Nose!! Kiss my nose! Up your nose!"

There is a sad postscript to all of this, which is that in the name of tolerance and understanding the Free Speech Movement has become so successful we may have lost more than we gained. For I find I am left with nothing to use profane enough, obscene enough, to describe the stupid waste and tragic death of Lenny Bruce.

ON THE STUMP

anyone
who would want the job
who would allow themselves
and their family
to go through
what they know
they must go through
to get the job

is clearly someone
we should
never let
anywhere near the job

OUTSIDE THE BOX

America desperately needs
to spend some time in its own shadow
acquainting itself
with how a have-not nation must feel
constantly having to kowtow to the power we wield!
never mind billions spent on foreign aid
beneficiaries abhor their benefactors
each gift a nagging reminder of one's inadequacies
secretly the French resent and hate us
for hauling their ass out of two world wars

so forget the past
9/11 and a handful of terrorists changed all that
the stock response to such a provocative attack
is suddenly and totally passé
as the thin red line of the British will attest
we won our independence the coward's way
shooting from ambush was simply not fair play

so what do we do with the likes of Osama bin Laden?
imprisonment? — execution? — assassination?
options that would only serve to create a martyr
his twisted convictions becoming
an even more compelling rallying point.
yet to do nothing but turn the other cheek
would work only with those of like mind
time for some thoughts
from outside the box

like
capturing bin Laden alive
our medical establishment working him over
and I mean over
removing facial hair — breast implants —
remodeling his genitals — blonding his tresses
and then in a tight-fitting cocktail dress
she's shoved out of a chopper to parachute
back into the heart of Afghanistan

the Taliban terrorist may be willing to commit suicide
for his fundamentalist belief
but face punishment this diabolically clever?
and risk becoming a woman?
Never!

THE DIVINE WIND

human nature being what it is —
the military arsenal being what it has become —
questions arise

backed into the same desperate corner
would a Napoleonic paperhanger
commit suicide these days?
or apocalypse?

pushed to the brink
do you think a fanatic Arab terrorist
would surrender unconditionally
to a Capitalist pig? — or vice versa?

the fact is an atheist might be less inclined
to blow up the here and now
than those among us who believe
in the sweet by-and-by

there is no defense
against a Kamikaze fundamentalist
willing to die flying prophecy
down the smokestack of human existence

even so
the heavyweights pose and bristle
confident as battleships
while dissidents on both sides
are ordered to get their thinking straight

"An eye for an eye!" the zealot shouts
"Pluck it out!" and never mind
that the whole world goes blind

PEACE PARADE

I ain't afraid to step in your bitter streets
And walk away from war.
I ain't afraid though the boulevard's full of heat
And hate — an open sore.
I ain't afraid, I ain't afraid
Ain't afraid of the hate I see
But when I see all the hate in me
I'm afraid.

I ain't afraid to face the red-neck wrath
And meet their savage need.
I won't run, let 'em come and block the path
I ain't afraid to bleed.
I ain't afraid, I ain't afraid,
Ain't afraid and that's a fact
But when I find I want to hit 'em back
I'm afraid

I ain't afraid of that hard mean-eyed cop
With his hand-carved billy-stick.
Ain't afraid when the bull-horns buzz and pop
"Liberals, don't you try no tricks!"
I ain't afraid, I ain't afraid,
Ain't afraid of none of this
But when I feel my hand become a fist
I'm afraid.

I ain't afraid to march to a public park
With peace symbols over my head.
And join with a few to protest the dark,
Call me yellow, call me red.
I ain't afraid, I ain't afraid
Ain't afraid of the hate in you
But when I find that I can hate too
I am afraid.

PEELING THE ONION

hey Buel
did you hear how Flash
got himself a dashiki and an Afro-wig?
I could dig it if he weren't Scotch-Irish
poor ol' Flash tried to break the mirror
and cut himself on the glass

he put me through a trick though
because I never went uptight
when Old Black Joe burnt himself
putting lye in his hair
trying to be white

the onion is all skins, Buel
and I am an onion
and as I keep discovering
and you keep pointing out
I am also a white racist...
so what do we do now?

well, I don't know about you
but being as how
I've got nothing better to do
I'll just pass the time peeling the onion
laughin' at the tears

Buel
do you think that you and I
black and white will ever learn how
to sit down and really relate
to a dwarf?

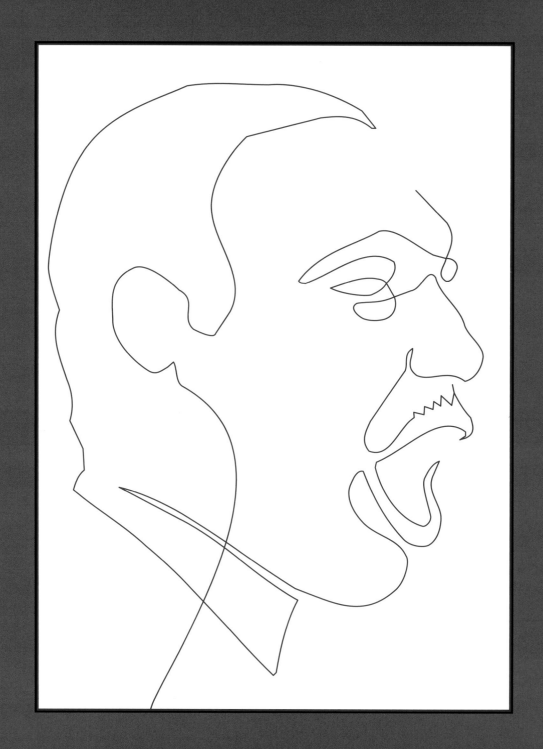

WHEN GIANTS PASS

me in 1963: "Martin Luther King?
Oh, isn't he the guy they keep putting in jail
for disturbing the peace?"

from here somehow
by a route too circuitous to detail
I come around
in the close dusky atmosphere
of Bethel Baptist
abruptly aware of surroundings
minus the glare of light off white skin
feeling conspicuous...
unable to conform
I bob on the surface
of the dark moist murmuring warm

what the visiting preacher
said there that evening remains a blur
yet I vividly recall the shoe
being on the other foot
and exactly
where in that packed assembly hall
the two other white faces were

afterward, at the reception
I observe the guest of honor
being shyly avoided
no one goes near him at all
he stands alone
looking tired and incredibly small
so I go up to the man and in a well-meaning
good-natured show business way
clap him on the back saying
"Working you pretty hard, are they?"

I still can't believe
I said that to Martin Luther King
and neither could he
looking up sharply
at such a blatant display of naiveté...
then with patience and remarkable grace
said simply
"Yes -— but it's worth it"

I tell this story
in much the same way Jubal George Taylor
my grandfather on my mother's side
described the day
when as a small boy
he stood with others by the railroad tracks
in a dismal gray rain
"I didn't know it then," he would say
"but I saw Abraham Lincoln's funeral train"

REVOLUTIONARY

I guess you'd call him
a revoultionary
but he laughed real laughter
and when he was quiet
his eyes were sad
so I hung around
to hear what he had to say

he said
we have broken the ocean beyond repair
the crabs are leaving
we will soon follow

he said
we live in an insane asylum
where the sensitive go insane
that is to say go sane
but then must kill the pain
with bottle and needle

he said
the next time the conquering heroes arrive
the future is gone in a nuclear flash

he said
and there is no time left for the corn
to grow

but the fact that he bothered to get out of bed
this morning and say it, gives me
a kind of hope

chapter 4

Fun & Games

Sport and Interpersonal Communication

THE QUESTION

the shirt sleeve was empty
folded neatly
and pinned up

obviously my eyes had saucered
because the wiry old man
cranked his grizzled head
in my direction
"You look like a lad full of questions,"
he said
"So I'll let you have one,
   but only one,
   so make it count, kid."

and of course I blurted out
"What happened to your arm, Sir?"

he leaned over to cough and spit
and then he straightened up
the hint of a twinkle
betraying his flinty stare
saying

"It got bit off."

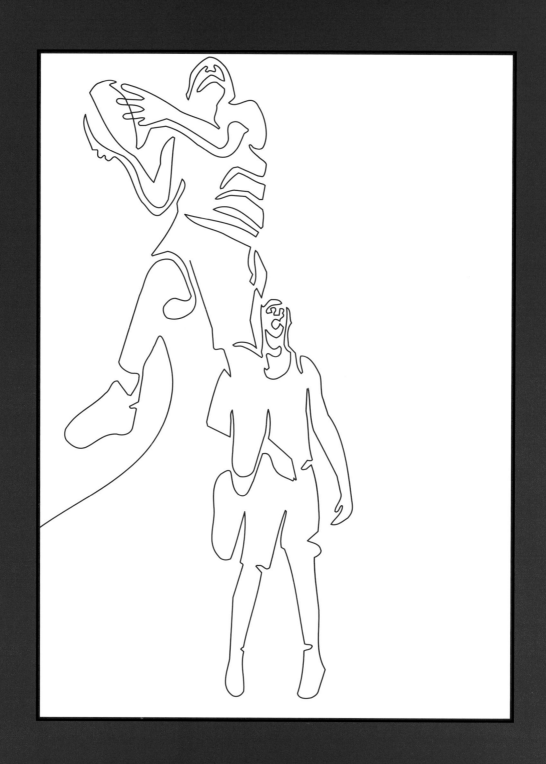

SECOND HALF

I turned forty a while ago
and came dribbling out of the locker room
ready to start the second half
glancing up at the scoreboard
I saw that we were behind
7 to 84
and it came to me then
            we ain't gonna win
and considering the score
I'm beginning to be damn glad
this particular game
ain't gonna go on forever

but don't take this to mean
I'm ready for the showers
take it to mean I'm probably gonna play
one helluva second half

now, I told this to some kids
in the court next to mine
and they laughed
but I don't think they understood
            how could they
playing in the first quarter
only one point behind

deep into autumn
the third period
I have discovered
that winning the game
is not what is important

what is important though
is
that I look good while losing

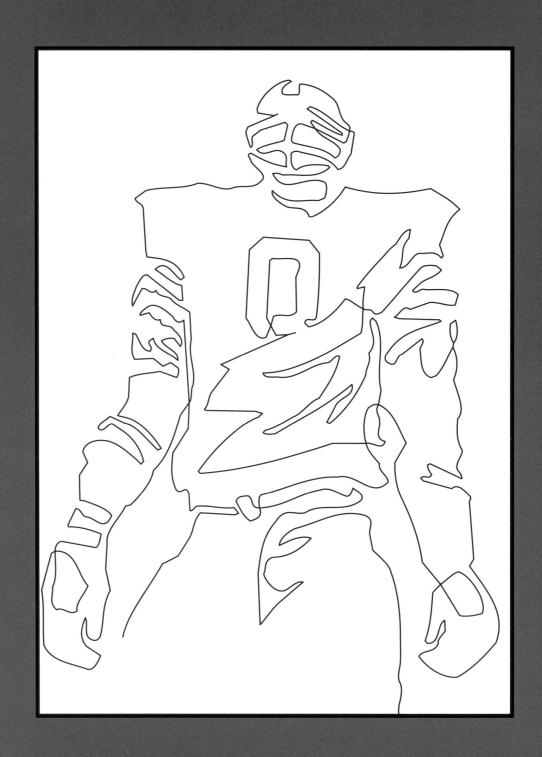

FOR SUCH A BRUTAL PRIMITIVE SPORT
I MUST APOLOGIZE

ladies
I hate to admit it
but there are times when I find
I haven't completely resigned
from the Neanderthal club
old Og
still needs a way to deal
with pent-up aggression
explaining perhaps
why the trip to the Super Bowl
has become such a national
obsession

but then
isn't it more humane and genteel
to tame the beast vicariously?
to sit
harmlessly watching a field
where padded paid professionals
hit and flog each other?
isn't this better
than taking it out on the wife
the kids
the dog and your mother?
to say nothing
about just possibly reducing
the risk of World War III?

ladies
I put it to you
isn't football
really
the civilized thing to do?

A HUNDRED YARDS OF CLICHÉS

on any given Sunday
a classic match-up
with play-off implications
and here to cover the action
a man who needs no introduction
before an overflow crowd
the gladiators take the field
it should be a high-scoring affair
the weather not a factor
the smell of upset in the air

10

his foot meets the ball
the pigskin is rooted a mile
fielded cleanly
a world-class sprinter
scoots up the alley
cuts back against the grain
runs into a brick wall
the zebras unscramble the pile
shaking the cobwebs away
he'll think about that for awhile

20

barking out the signals
he takes the snap
sees some daylight – ka-pow!
the big guy closes the door
it depends on where they spot the ball
the chain gang comes in
too early to gamble
turning it over they boot it away
it's a game of inches
and both teams came to play

30

lost in the sun
coughing it up
digging it out of the dirt
he'll have to eat it right there
they dodged a bullet that time
the field general goes to work
the men in the trenches stay home
earning their keep
it's a physical sport
and nothing comes cheap

40

marching down the field
flags flying
that'll come back to haunt 'em
they come away empty
great protection
relentless pursuit
goose eggs up on the score board
the outcome remains a mystery
the seconds tick away
the first half is history

50

it's back to the drawing board
conferring with the men upstairs
making the adjustments
changing the game plan
they know they're in a ball game now
rallying the troops
I wonder what he's telling them in there?
the 2nd half holds the answer
and while waiting for play to resume
a word from our sponsor

40

they come right out firing
throwing up the bomb
going for all the marbles
dodging the sack
he scrambles around in the pocket
connecting for a bundle
on a roll
reaching into his bag of tricks
it's the old Statue of Liberty
chalk up a quick six

30

the extra point goes astray
a kicker's life is a lonely one
mistakes will kill you
fielding the pumpkin he breaks one loose
motoring from coast to coast
it's a brand new ball game now
splitting the uprights they go on top
the momentum swings
but there's lots of time left on the clock
it ain't over 'til the fat lady sings

20

a seesaw battle
an all-out war
the crowd is beside itself
what they need now is a score
an immaculate reception
he goes to the shotgun
they come with the blitz
it goes down to the wire
a Hail Mary at the gun
pulling a squeaker out of the fire

10

you do what you have to do
go with what got you there
it was a barn-burner
they simply didn't have the horses
all hands can stand tall
someone wins — someone loses
that's the name of the game
you go out and give it your all
no question about it
that's football

(What's the score?
Answer in artwork.)

WIDOWS OF THE NFL

during the season
do not arrange social engagements
unless you have checked with him first
all dates are in doubt
Sundays are sacred of course
but since Monday-night-football
is often played on Thursday
rational thinking is out

and don't try to circumvent this
by inviting friends over
to watch the game with your spouse
if they root for the other city
the scene in the den will not be pretty
and probably end
with a SWAT team surrounding your house
however
if the cheering section is compatible
do plan to serve snacks during the action
not hor d'oeuvres — nothing fancy like that
just be sure to include something
from the five major food groups
caffeine alcohol sugar salt and fat

and don't assume
he's enjoying himself in there
rabid football fans are perpetually wretched
touchdowns ahead they still feel defeated
convinced that they can't keep the lead
down by a point and it's hopeless
"we'll never score what we need!"

and it is really okay for a woman
to hate the game
better this than pretending to be a fan
a "sports buddy"
with a bright inquiring mind
trying to impress him with questions
about nickel-backs and point-spread
as he watches his team fall a field goal behind

but most of all
after the opening whistle has blown
don't get sexy
studies have shown that football
renders a man impotent
at game time don't try to touch the remote
besides you have your own hands-off policy
during Law & Order
and Murder She Wrote

keep in mind though
the road to the Super Bowl may seem endless
but a frustrated maid must not lose faith
as she lies alone in her bed
when the Pro Bowl is over
so is the season
and the couch potato will rise from the dead

THE GRAND PIANO MAN

Dedicated to Jonathan Lee

Later — down the road a piece
Somewhere far from that
Misty morning at Big Sur
The crowd rippling with excitement
Then the gun — and you begin the run
Effortless at first
Graceful curves — easy straight-aways
Highway One a paved treadmill
Rolling under your flying feet

Then abruptly
The grueling long hard pull
Out of Little Sur up to Hurricane Point
At the top, flagged and exhausted
You round a sharp bend
And run smack into a panoramic view
Better still — the inclination is down
A brisk wind washes your face
Combs your hair
And there is something else charging
The electric air — Music!
Radiating up from Bixby Bridge

Loping down the sloping road
You cross that majestic viaduct and
Waiting on the other side
The grand piano man
Passing out cups of cool concerto
To splash on your fatigue
Refresh your resolve

Continuing on
Over miles of ups and downs
Past outlooks and vistas
Through the Highland's piney woods
And then the ecstasy
Of crossing the finish line
Where bent over, hands on knees
You catch your breath and get your time

But later — reflecting back on all of this
Music will be the first thing
That comes to mind — like a life metaphor
Waiting just on the other side
Of that concrete span
There is — and there will always be
A grand piano man

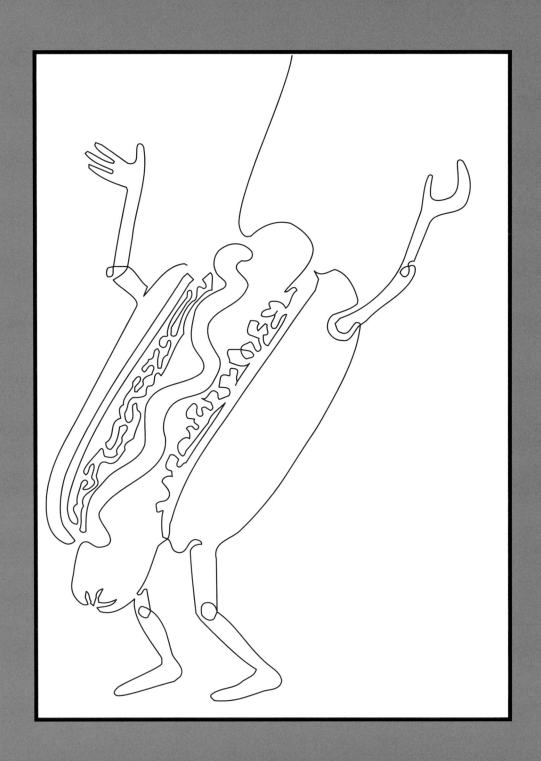

STRESS

I have just hung up the telephone
but the bad news will have to wait

right now
I must deal with the lump of tension
that has just
been thrust into my body
like a frankfurter into a sliced roll

stuffed with stress
my own intestine
swells like a boiled sausage
till it gets all the mustard and relish
leaving the leavened bread
the staff of life
stuck with a red-hot

as a creative person
I try to be thankful
for the sudden presence
of this annoying intruder
knowing
that a gut full of anxiety
can be a useful motivator
and knowing also
that a bun all by itself
would never make it
at Coney Island

and certainly
I want to make it
I'd love to be
an Oscar Meyer wiener
singing and dancing
a real hot-dog!

but that doesn't mean
I enjoy being eaten

MEN – MISSING THE MARK

yes,
even sharp shooters like Sergeant York
missed occasionally
and I'm told
by certain female intimates
that all across the civilized world
women have mopped muttering
if the target is that hard to hit
why can't a man making his stand
just sit?

however women
a musketeer's aim and marksmanship
are not the problem here
as in the game of darts
dead center is NOT
where the big points are scored...
it's the half-inch of — (silence)
at the edge of the pond
the thin strip of porcelain... .

> [Believe it or not ladies,
> every man is a crack shot,
> it's just that
> in attempting to be soft-spoken
> we zero in on the spot
> where the water isn't
> and check it out, there's not much
> where the water isn't.
> and it's way out at the edge]

even an expert
flirting this way with the rim
can't be expected to keep all of his darts
on the board...
I don't know who made up the rules
or why

but for some reason Prudence
prefers the hush of the hard surface
to the voice of the laughing pool

> [Think about it, folks, everyone knows
> what you're doing in there....
> They do it in there themselves....
> So why is it you would rather die
> than be heard doing what you know
> they know you're doing?]

it makes no sense at all
considering
the symphony we go through
whistling and coughing
and clearing our throats
when intruders approach in the hall
why not simply
let 'em know we're in there
with the sweet sound of a waterfall?

now there's a liberating thought!
from this day forward
I shall let the work speak for itself
and by so doing
show some real concern
for the clean-up crew
killing two birds with one stone
my sights as well
as my consciousness raised

I for one will blaze away
at the bulls-eye
a welcome visitor
known by women the world over
as a straight shooter

KINDERGARTEN LOGIC

how many mornings have I struggled
on the forest floor
trying to pull my pants on
inside a sleeping bag?

cursing and muttering
in the darkness of that collapsible hole
looking for all the world
like some stricken giant green bug
writhing on the ground
in its death throes

this morning I awoke clear-headed
and decided to stand like a man
and do it the easy way
and I did
and was steppin' into 'em
just as slick as you please
when I heard this voice whispering

someone will see you!

and in the chilly early-morning air
of that crowded campground
I stood there
pants half-mast
and thought about that
and it came to me
in a blinding flash
the reason
we don't offer a course in logic
to kindergarten kids

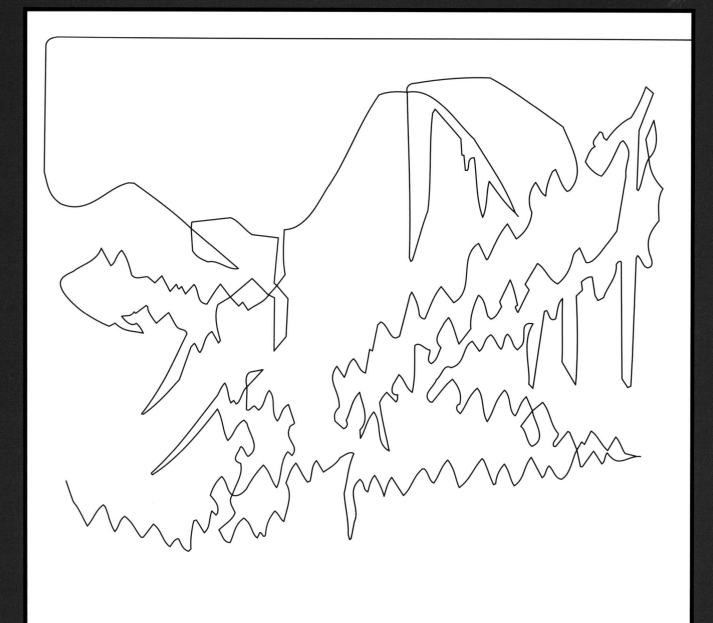

IN DEFENSE OF GOING BALD

"Getting a little thin on top
 aren't you sport?"
my Neanderthal brothers get a kick
out of razzing me this way
and I am going bald
but what would you have me do?
nurture and cultivate a sideburn
till it hangs down like a house plant
a long trailing fern
to rake across my barren crown

or would you prefer a transplant
my naked pate a parade ground
where rows of foreign follicles
stand stiffly like the Michigan State
marching band
poised to play the national anthem

perhaps a toupée?
a saucy little pompadour
that when not in use
lies around the house like a lap dog
like the dusty pelt of a Pekingese
which I suspect smells of musty tapestry

do this to my head? no way — not me!

like the granite dome
that presides over Yosemite Valley
I would not be what I am with trees
my scalp is bare
but gentlemen look at it this way
we all begin with roughly
the same number of hormones
and if you want to blow yours
growing hair….?

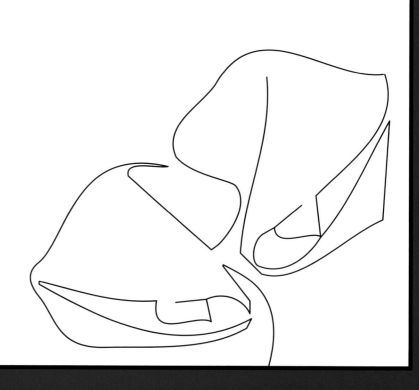

FORTUNE COOKIES

with a kind of early Mickey Rooney
Judy Garland innocence
we go before the church and state
exchanging unspoken trust
for legal documents the sole intent of which
is meant to cover and protect
all moonstruck lovers from themselves
when later in the course of human events
comes the expected divorce
and property settlement

the magic and excitement traded off
for false security — signed — sealed
and written down — the guarantee
that neither he nor she will ever sneak around

and didn't we go down beneath the weight
of that iron-clad bouquet
dead
preserved in the state of wed-LOCK
and is it any wonder
that pickled in this atmosphere
the act of love becomes a habit
like eating in a Chinese restaurant
only because it's close and handy
sitting down together with the empty sound
of clicking chop sticks
and nothing left between
but pork chow mein and strained silence
the bill always coming
with fortune cookie wisdom
like
"He who catches bus
will never have to chase it."

and other sad commentaries
written by some poor sap and his wife
trapped forever in a cookie factory
on the outskirts of every city and town
in America

CONVERSATION

I have just wandered back
 into our conversation
and find that you are still rattling on
about something or other
I think I must have been gone
at least twenty minutes
and you never missed me

now this might say something
about my acting ability
or it might say something about
your sensitivity

one thing troubles me though
when it is my turn
to rattle on for twenty minutes
which I have been known to do
have you been missing too?

ODE TO A REMOVABLE PARTIAL DENTURE

feigning nonchalance
like an adolescent
purchasing a prophylactic
I furtively
bought a tube of Fixodent today

a disturbing experience
although I am no stranger to the realm
of crowns bridges and caps...
remove the fixed frontal facades
and I'm left with nothing
but pegs notches and gaps
the sunny smile you see
is not the one I displayed in youth
but once the dentist's artistry
is cemented down
and the tongue wearies of exploration
one tends to forget the truth

receding hairline
trifocals – liver spots
all have been taken in stride
but not this recent oral acquisition
this sculpted wire amalgam
barbed and hooked where it bends
pink cocktail olives
stuffed with ivory pimentos
skewered at both ends

in place it magically fits in
but on the counter top — in the sink
it appears sinister
like some gleaming
surgical device
left here by intruders
from outer space
perhaps
an instrument of torture
dating from the Inquisition
my natural exuberance
curbed
by this cruel Spanish bit

and to think
for the rest of my life
I must play host
to this illusive parasite
this spiny-finned pilot fish
watching it
dart in and out of my mouth
knowing that
it is secretly holed up
somewhere in there
waiting to eat

and although
it does feel good
to dine with molars again
symbolically
the moment this metallic interloper
was parked in my mouth
marked for me
the beginning of the end

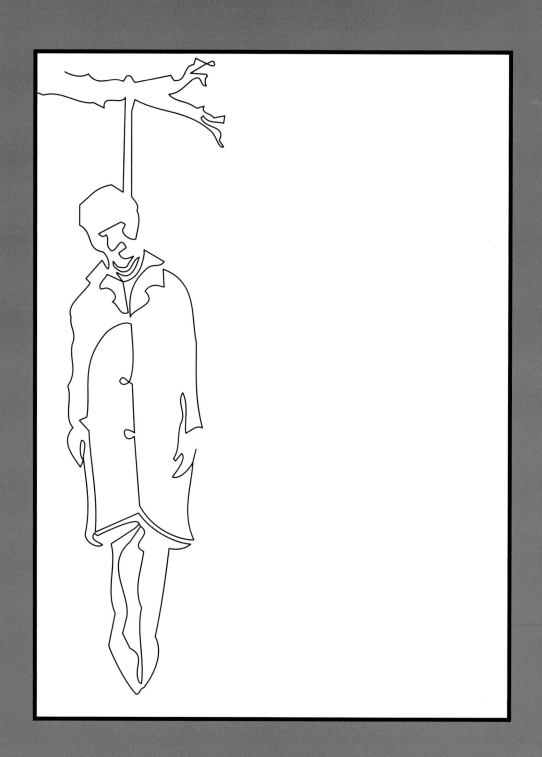

MEDICINE HAT

You're in the town of Medicine Hat,
It's the year of the drought.
Out on the bone dry prairie
Death walked all about.
The sun boiled up the river,
Your cattle die of thirst,
The crops are burned and withered,
No, things can't get much worse.

Then to the town of Medicine Hat
Came a rain-makin' man.
Said for a thousand dollars
He would save the land
He'd bring the rain asplashin'
Like magic from the sky.
So you scrape to raise the cash
And you pay the man to try
And make rain,
Gentle rain, blessed rain.

The rainmaker gets a drum
And he commences to pound.
He sets a pot to boilin'
Till the steam churned all around.
Fills a sack with horntoads,
Paints a line across the ground,
But not a sign of rain
As the sun went down.

Outside the town of Medicine Hat,
Just before it was dawn,
You catch him with your money
He was movin' on.
You need no judge and jury,
He's guilty as can be,
So you string him up in fury
Out at the hanging tree.

A man was hung in Medicine Hat,
And as the rope stretched tight,
A soft wind started blowin'
Rain clouds into sight.
You'd hung a cheat and a faker
Yet you are filled with shame
As you bury the rainmaker
And walk home in the rain
Gentle rain, blessed rain.

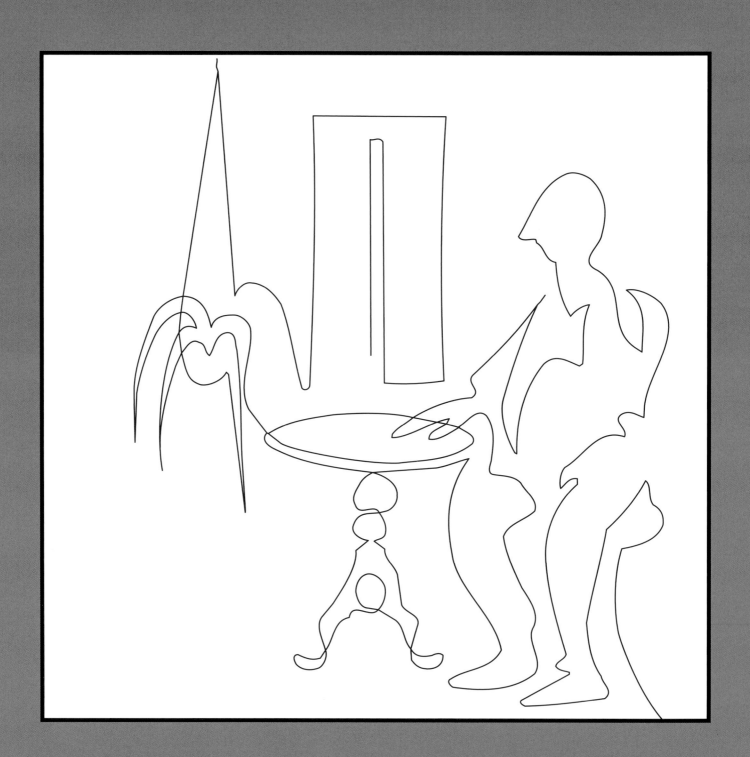

SANCTUARY

at the dental clinic
it was standing-room only
the patients caught up in *Time*
peering at *People*
the lucky ones
fighting in the Middle East
and reviewing the latest movies
keeping themselves once removed
from the grim receptionist
who called out our names
one by one like death

and I
a candidate for a root canal
with nothing left in the magazine rack
but *House Beautiful*
and a dozen copies of *Dental Digest*

well you do what you can
with what you've got
and pictured on page 54
was a bare room
completely unfurnished
except for a bright green air-fern
hanging beside a stark white
wrought-iron ice-cream table
and chair

and it was there that I sat
bristling
glaring at the man
who had *The New Yorker*

A FARM ACCIDENT YEARS AGO

the horses shied and then wild-eyed
bolted from the field
racing back toward the barn
traces flying
the mower still attached
and running close behind
your father shouting an alarm
as that ugly snapping arm
reached out
taking everything off at the ankle
weeds and corn and hollyhock
and then in slow motion
sweeping through the stems
of two small boys frozen in surprise

and sometime later
in a photograph we find
those grinning little peg-legged Petes
proud as punch
posing

though the color and shape
are exactly right
an artificial limb is what it is
and can be put on and taken off
but the story that comes with it
walks
and walks and walks

chapter 5

Words For Survival

More from the Prostate Cancer Odyssey

THE PRESS
AND THE PRESIDENTIAL POLYP
(Not the one on his nose, the one at the other end)

suddenly the mind of America
focuses
on the place where the sun never shines

like characters
in a George Lukas movie
we are hurtled down a mile of twisting colon
light from the flexible sigmoidoscope
probing ahead
till rounding an undulating corner
I half expect to see Indiana Jones
cracking his whip —
leaning against an abnormal outcropping
a devil-may-care smile on his face

all the time Dan Rather
like a Grayline tour guide
calling out points of interest
carefully explaining that the bowels
in which we were trespassing
were not actually the President's —
talk about an invasion of someone's privacy!

of course
for the delighted proctologist
it was all money in the bank
but for those of us who blanch
at the thought of a rubber glove
snapping!
afraid to chance a medical checkup
for fear of what the doctor might find
believe me
these have been difficult times

I mean
if the Commander and Chief's villous adenoma
can go undetected
what hope do the rank and file have

it would seem then
that an unrestrained press
has once again left the American public
en masse
with a quizzical finger up its collective —

ANNUAL CHECKUP

every now and then
I discover this strange lump
in my abdomen which I finger
when no one is looking
to see if the soreness is still there
and it always is
so in fear and trembling
I go to see my doctor
to hear the bad news
and this kindly old bird
hops around me
like a crow with a piece of tin foil
poking and peering
until stroking his chin
he declares
that I am in A-1 condition
and if I'd stop handling my pancreas
it wouldn't be so sore

and yet always in the end
I leave his office
with the certain knowledge
that I will be dead in six months
the good doctor
keeping my awful infirmities from me
so that I could enjoy
what little time I have left
and bravely with this information
hidden under my coat
I return home to be with my family
and together
we climb the hill in back of the house
to sit a spell
and really watch a cloud move.

I guess you'd say
I was a bit of a hypochondriac
and that's OK
it keeps me close to things
and on this ward we are all
terminal anyway

PHARAOH AND THE MAN OF LA MANCHA

recently
I have lost two friends
David, the young one
succumbing to suicide
and Chuck, in his late sixties,
losing a long and grueling
battle with prostate cancer
the irony is obvious

here we have David not quite forty
everything going for him
and opting out
the determined victim
of a bout with melancholy
unwilling to face even one more day
David frozen in lifeless repose
reclining on his king-size motel bed
another in the sad procession
of young dead Pharaohs

then Chuck grayed and grizzled
man of La Mancha
painfully forcing himself to rise
from his sickbed each morning
to tilt with extinction
Chuck ferociously clinging to breath
wringing it out for every
precious moment he could get
stubbornly doing this
until unhorsed at last
he reluctantly faded

Chuck and David
David and Chuck
in death such diverse cases
if only they could have met in life
and traded places

MAN AMONG MEN

in a note thanking me
for sharing my
Prostate Cancer Odyssey
she wrote
my husband….
my ex-husband….
the only husband I ever had
I'm not sure
what to call him now
I'm only certain that
he was a man
among men
who "didn't want to know"

Lennie is — was — his name
and for many years
I begged him to see a doctor
about the pain in his gut
the chronic weakness
and wobbly legs
that wrecked his tennis game
I hoped his love of tennis
might prompt him
to go to the Doc…. but no

he died of prostate cancer
it spread and grew in Lennie
the way untreated latter day
cancer can grow
and then he knew
and now he's gone

chalk up
one more man among men
who "didn't want to know"

THE WAGON MASTER SYNDROME

I often find myself wandering around
in the wrong century
a stage coach pony express kind of guy
having to constantly explain why
I'd rather die than see the saw bones

I don't need no bespectacled old geezer
thumping – peering
and putting his cold stethoscope on me
ain't no gunslinger worth his salt
puts up with sissy claptrap like that?
no-sir-ee!

what kind of wagon master
would scare the women and children
telling them the Comanche
is out there just over the next hill?
or that his belly constantly aches
only yeller-streak cowards
talk about being frightened and ill
when a Texas Ranger
steps forward in the wild West
best he keep a tight lip
and a flinty glint in his eye

can you imagine a circle
of leather-faced cattle drovers
hunkered down around a prairie fire
spitting tobacco juice
discussing erectile dysfunction
and what brand of diaper
incontinent men should use

out here
on the modern medical frontier
the prairie schooners have all disappeared
and no one I know ever had one
so what kind of a man still adheres
to the wagon master syndrome?

... a dead one!

THE OSTRICH

after the original diagnosis and treatment
I became the classic "ostrich"
head thrust deep in the sand of denial
I did my best
to keep myself in the dark
and during
that blind unattended time
my disease sneaks up on me
morphing into the very aggressive
de-differentiated neuroendocrine carcinoma
the label alone
being a head's up eye opener!
at long last I faced the fact
that the ostrich cannot fly
time to take an active role
in my fight for survival
time to look the demon in the eye

so I go on line where dumb luck
and a benevolent "search engine"
find the Prostate Cancer Research Institute
I dial the "helpline"
and for more than an hour
an anonymous Good Samaritan
calmly slows me down until
my philosophy of life can catch up
and begin to see me through.

once again I'm able to recall
that only where the path of difficulty
crosses the easy way
can growth and change occur
that the height of my highest high
is in direct proportion
to the depth of my deepest down
lessons I'd lost sight of
when my butt was in the sky
and my brains were underground

REGARDING DOCTORS
ON GOOD DAYS AND BAD DAYS

In turn I've met them all
Doctors Slash, Poison & Burn

on good days
my urologist is Arthur of Camelot
wielding Excalibur in my defense
Zorro, foiling enemy lesions
a deft dashing master of surgery
on bad days — Jack the Ripper!
stropping an edge on his flashing blade
Sweeny Todd intent on doing butchery
Genghis Khan hacking and chopping
his way through me

on good days
my oncologist is Merlin wise and kind
dispenser of healing elixirs
the Lone Ranger coming to the rescue
leaving silver bullets behind
on bad days — Dr. Jeckel!
with unexpected side effects to Hyde
like the cackling witch in Snow White
he stirs his bubbling cauldron
feeding me apples with venom inside

on good days
my radiologist is Keeper of the Fire
Shaman — squire of healing beams
firing off therapeutic volleys
the Buck Rogers of my dreams
on bad days — Dr. Strangelove!
fondling his arsenal of bombs
Nero fiddling...fanning the flames
and if General Sherman is on the march
then Georgia is my name

in closing
I suppose it's obvious
and goes without
my having to say
that these contrary lines
were composed
on a very very bad day

153

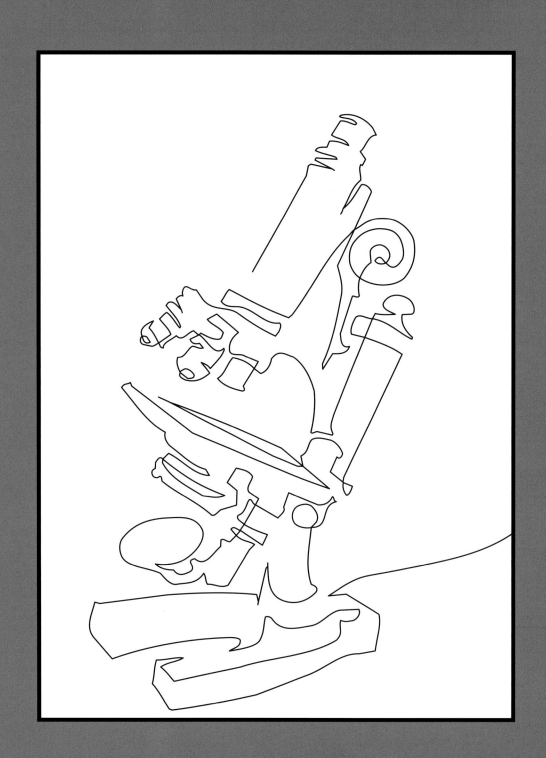

PSA DREAD

the battle
with the "Big C" monster
is scored by the numbers
like a jury trial
digits sequester and deliberate
bringing in a verdict every six weeks
under a microscope the blood I bled
is analyzed — the evidence scrutinized
the side-effect of these proceedings
PSA dread

in capital cases such as mine
the deliberations never end
and over time I've been both
acquitted and condemned
the only constant being
the tide of apprehension
that ebbs and flows
invisible as air — in my belly
in my brain — even seeping
into positive lab results
PSA dread

shackled to trepidation
I willingly take the stand
to share the experience with others
publicly bearing witness
with pencil in hand I'm able to stare
the prosecutor down and free myself
with the cutting edge
of testimony like this

I wanted in the worst way
to put elephants and trying not
to think about them
in bed with PSA dread
but by the time I chased
the punch line down
there wasn't an elephant
left in my head

and this is how I survive
this is why I am still alive

THE EVANGELIST

lived experience has taught them
most of what they know
so MDs treating men
diagnosed with hormone refractory
advanced prostate cancer
automatically put us on death row
and taking the past into account
this negativity is understandable...
these good-hearted doctors
watch us come and go
honestly doing what they can
like kindly prison guards
attempting to make the life
we have left as pleasant as possible

to be otherwise a physician
would have to be a bit delusional
evangelical even...
to work so diligently for
and believe so fervently in the concept
of the last-minute reprieve

for those of us
confined on cell block PC
doing time
with an executioner stalking
it is exhilarating to find
an oncologist
willing to fly in the face of history
refusing to call the likes of me
"Dead man walking."

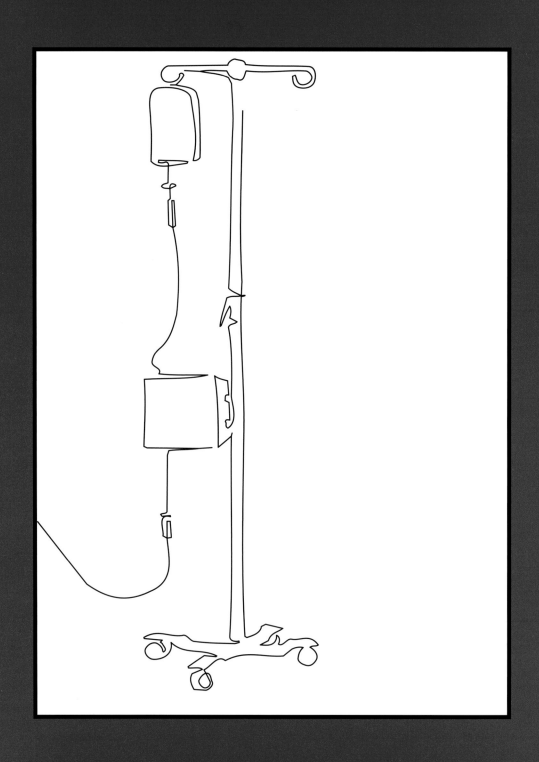

THE HOUSE OF DRIPS

there is an address
on El Dorado
where I go and climb the stairs
I've learned to get there early
before clients fill the chairs
It's best to be the first
whose name is sweetly paged
before these lovely working girls
have all become engaged

gathered in the parlor
beauties one and all
and I never know which cutie
will lead me down the hall
but it really doesn't matter
all are deft at what they do
so let the act of drawing straws
determine
who accesses who

when Vivian steps forward
I know my day is made
you'll notice she's left-handed
as she plies her trade
and I'm filled
with expectations
as I open shirt and vest
for Vivian's corpus callosum
is larger than the rest

Allison, tall and slender
she gets my second look
she says
when she's not working
she curls up with a book
she once did
something extra
I mean, at my request
so Allison instructed me
to pay at the front desk
    (flu shot)
and Nora,
that Irish beauty
speaks with an Irish brogue
me thinks that Nora thinks
I'm a "wee bit of a rogue"
but I surmise she's drawn to me
like gravy to a spud
for Nora loves to needle me
until
she draws my blood

and Lindy,
laughing Lindy
let me tell you she's the one
'cause every time she does me
she make it loads of fun
when Lindy runs the session
it gives me such a rush
to have her
waltz into the room
and give my port a flush

I call
and make appointments
like every other John
it's to the House of Drips I go
each week to get it on
with four oncology nurses
Yes, that's who this is about
the four angels of mercy
I cannot live without

THE NAVIGATORS

search engines now enable patients
to sail the waters of the World Wide Web
charting everything there is to know
about any given medical predicament

perhaps this is the reason doctors
no longer carry that little black bag
the one full of gleaming implements of cure
when all it really contained
was a jar full of leaches and an auger
for drilling holes in the skull
to let the demons out

elevate yourself
in the Chain of Command!
above physician and homeopath
especially when attempting to circumvent
a disease that "there is no right way to treat"
take over the helm! — don't cower below deck
stuck in steerage powerless and beaten

in the mid-eighteen hundreds
clipper-ship captains gathered in waterfront taverns
to quarrel and vie about the safest route
around Cape Horn and where to hide out
in the Straits of Magellan to ride out a storm

just so —
in prostate cancer circles
navigation still rules
as always the topic of conversation
the latest treatment — the promising trial

holding tight to the rigging
together we scan the horizon
hoping to see where some
medical genius has begun
digging the Panama Canal

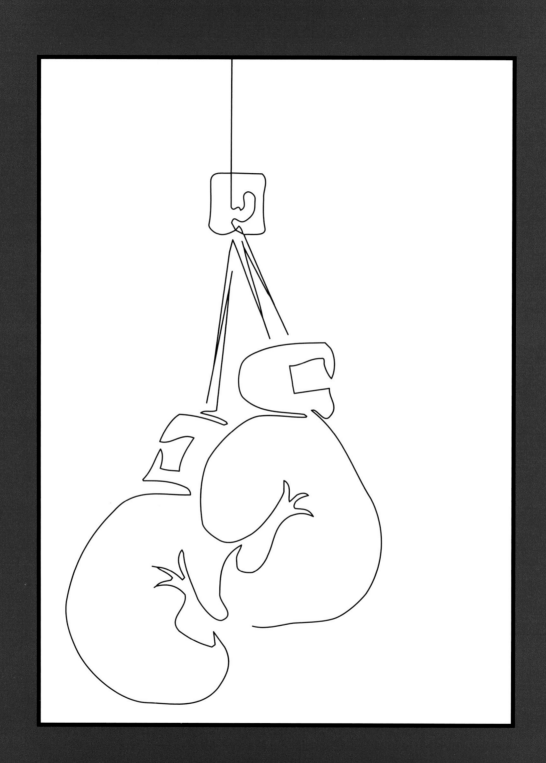

THE BOXER

I was deathly afraid
when the match was made
and it was determined that I
would be put in the ring
with this heavy-weight brawler
notorious mauler who has put
more than a few good men down
by comparison I'm a light-weight
a dip and dodger, bob and weaver
dancing my way through
the first two rounds

but like they say
"you can run but you can't hide"
this ruthless foe
raining blow after blow
through the third, the fourth and the fifth
"Keep counter punching!" my handlers yell
as I answer the bell for round six
fatigued — done in — worn out
and it's tough to keep slipping punches
in a bout you know you can't win
in a fight where the fix is in

at the moment I'm down on one knee
taking a breather
the referee counts Three! Four! Five!
I'm aware of the numbers
and staying alive but this time
I don't feel like bouncing back up
Six! Seven! Eight! I see the oncologist
in the morning at Nine!
tonight I write this and wait

LIKE RACCOONS

like raccoons we also wear a mask
but instinctively recognize our own kind
prostate cancer survivors
come to forage a "Treatment and Cure" lecture
the specialist winding up his remarks
with some thoughts on "Quality of Life"
and "Graceful Endings"
the "Newly Diagnosed" leaning forward
taking copious notes until the aforementioned
change of subject emptied the hall emotionally
swept it clean

"They just don't get it!" the specialist wept
"They don't want to know the road to Easter
  goes through Good Friday."

after dark raccoons materialize
at the Laguna Seca Speedway
searching for roadside snacks
crisscrossing highway and track
trapped suddenly in headlight glare
they freeze — petrified
ultrasound and biopsy results leaving
them scared stiff — eyes wide — jaws slack

but think about it boys — think about it
we're born — we live — we die
so what's different now? Not a thing!
except being blessed with a constant reminder
to never let another unexplored moment slip by

my condolences to those
who fall prey to the fatal surprise
the unexpected cardiac arrest
the sudden traffic casualty
forced to depart short of a conclusion
short of the all important "good-byes."

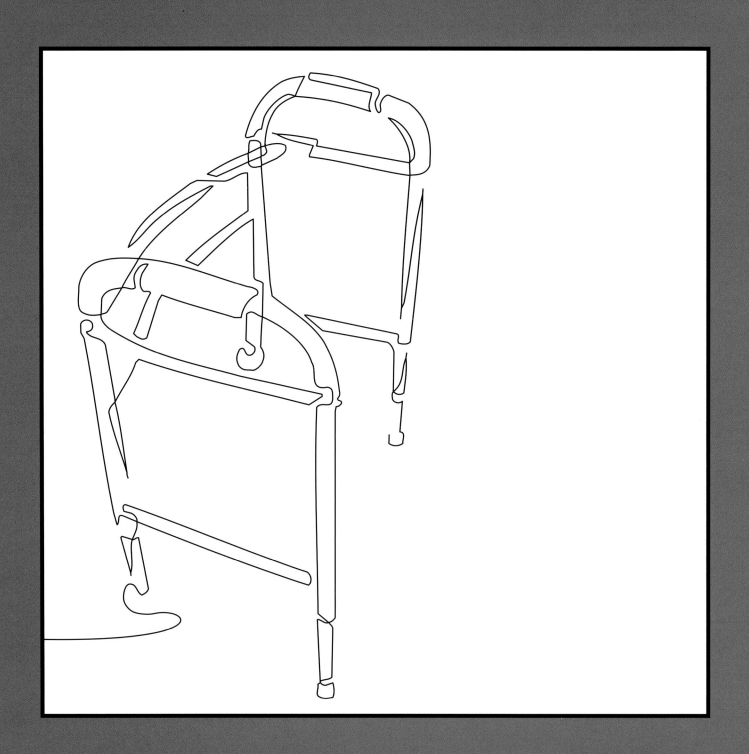

ABOUT TO BECOME AN ARTIFICIAL HIPSTER

I've been waiting since childhood
to become the "Bionic Man"
able to leap tall buildings
in a single bound!
no, that was Superman.
I want to be like that other guy.
you know, the six-million-dollar dude
the one in that old TV show
running fast/faster
with the "boing boing" sound track
resounding in the background

It's not that I
long to be a super hero
hanging out with the X-men
it's just that in these latter days
I'd like to lose the walker
and become a walker
myself
again

GARDEN UNDER SIEGE

Advanced Prostate Cancer Survival Strategy

*In order of importance
the Count Down from 10 to Number 1.*

10. Diagnosis "Crabgrass!" Saith the yardman,
     And chopping with his hoe the war began.

9. The invading horde continues to grow.
    Time to give the recommended herbicides a go.

8. Focusing in on persistent node and sprout.
   Incinerate, scorch, and burn the sucker out.

7. Test religiously, — Here, ignorance is not bliss.
   A wild refractory plant can deliver a death kiss.

6. Don't fixate on only killing this insidious weed.
   Fortify the soil to resist its root and seed.

5. Search for horticulturists, — Be cyber-smart.
   The internet has wisdom and knowledge to impart.

4. Spade in nothing crabgrass likes to eat.
   Be inhospitable as a slab of cold hard concrete.

3. Walk in the sunshine, it will help you convalesce.
   Do interludes of Tai Chi to quiet down the stress.

2. Take an interest in the other fellow's plight.
   Tell your story, — Share the details of your fight.

1. Dance in the now! — Even in this blight-infested space.
   This patch of weeds, — This most holy place.

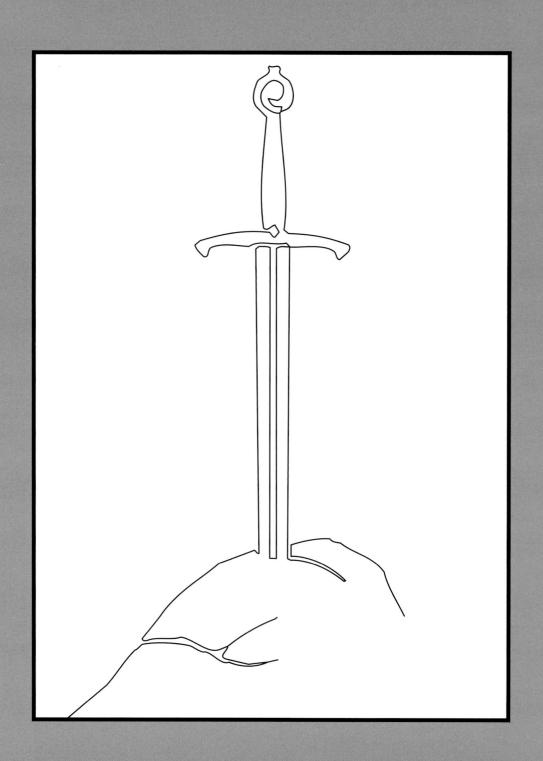

A WORD FOR SURVIVAL

(Dedicated to William Hoyt Jr.)

The man who coined the word
Had a terminal disease
A realist who knew that language
Strengthens, heals, and frees
Fear — the silent assassin
Will bring you to your knees
While faith can pull Excalibur
From stubborn stones with ease

The outcome of any illness
Is never absolute
No matter what the odds are
The end is always moot
It's only in uncertainty
That true hope can be found
And you can bet a sure thing
Will always let you down

He fought the "Big C" monster
With spunk and attitude
Another cockeyed optimist
You should not conclude
So like the fallen colors
I've taken up his word
And shout it from the hill top
Till the echo can be heard

He was no Pollyanna
His word no platitude
To things considered saccharine
He could be abrupt and rude
In the present-day vernacular
He was a righteous dude
Let's hear it for the man
Who coined the word
Spiritude!

chapter 6   # Happy Endings in the Badlands

Philosophy & Religion

PLASTIC PROPHET

it's 1969
and I'm telling about Bella my burro and me
and I'm telling about riding her barefoot
up Palo Colorado Canyon Road
where the afternoon sun
fell through the redwood canopy
in shafts of light
and about how I'm well aware
of the picture I am painting
religiously taking the time to pause
and pose in every slanted pillar and beam
and I'm telling about this hippie guy
who really did look like John the Baptist
and how I'm clippity cloppin' past him
face lifted to the light
when I hear this flat voice mumble excitedly:
"Jesus Christ!, it's Jesus Christ!"

then right in the middle of New York State
this Dead-Head type
hollers up at me on stage:
"You are plastic, man, you are SO plastic!"
and it was right about here that I nearly
fell off my burro and hurt myself

but then there is this to be said about plastic
everything is and everything isn't
and individually it's up to each of us
to decide which is what
so I decided to tell you
about me and my burro Bella
and to hell with it!

RAINBOW'S END

it was just a rundown truck stop
a greasy-spoon café
twenty years behind me now
seems like yesterday
I was on my way to somewhere
to pull off some big deal
like every kid of twenty
"the inventor of the wheel"
I had scrambled eggs and coffee
a piece of buttered toast
and the drivers at the counter
were more talkative than most

and when the subject wasn't women
they talked about the road
and the miles that they had traveled
and the weight of the load
funny... ain't it funny
how it all comes 'round again
it was just a roadside truck stop
and they called it Rainbow's End

and I sat there feelin' empty
as those poor devils spoke
if that was all there was to life
then it's a short length of rope
but remember I was twenty
and I've covered ground since then
I've picked-up on philosophy
a Greek became my friend
I've looked into religion
read Sartrees and Camoose
been up on the mountain
with an old guru

and when the subject isn't women
they talk about the road
and the miles that they had traveled
and the weight of the load
funny... ain't it funny
how it all comes 'round again
it was just a roadside truck stop
and they called it Rainbow
Zen

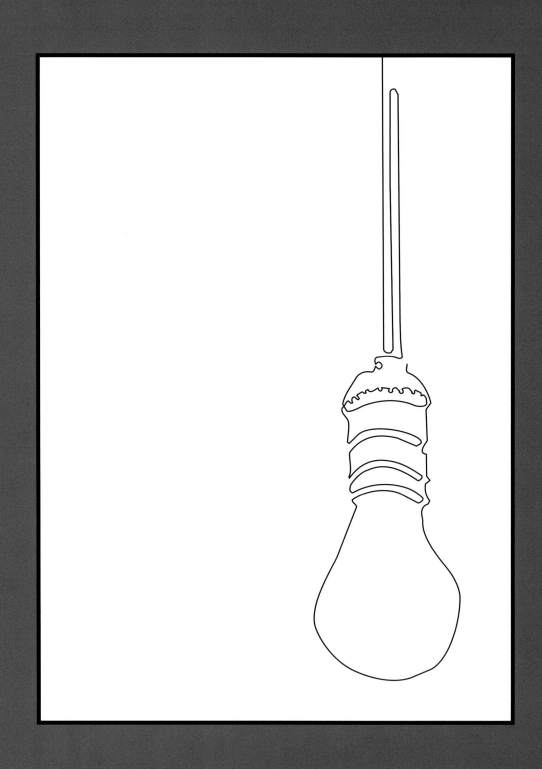

BACKSTAGE

I am often taken in
by the stagecraft pictured
on the pages of *Sunset* magazine
settings
that speak to me somehow saying
"in this breakfast nook
 you will never be lonely again"

and I should know better
I who reside in a theatrical set
that I propped up on the apron
of the Santa Lucia mountains

from the road
everything looks real enough
but I know that the walls
are made of painted rags
and the tower
sways in the breeze

on Sundays
they stream out from the city
passenger cars creeping by
people pointing
living for a moment in a poet's dream

I wave from the window
why not?
how could they know there's nothing
behind any of this
nothing except
what they bring to it themselves
this is not to say
that in this living space
there are not those rare moments
when we gather on the deck
to see a crescent moon at sunset
the air alive
with the sound of Rainbirds
whispering down in the garden

but
in the theater
when the audience goes home
there is always that one
unblinking naked light bulb left on
backstage

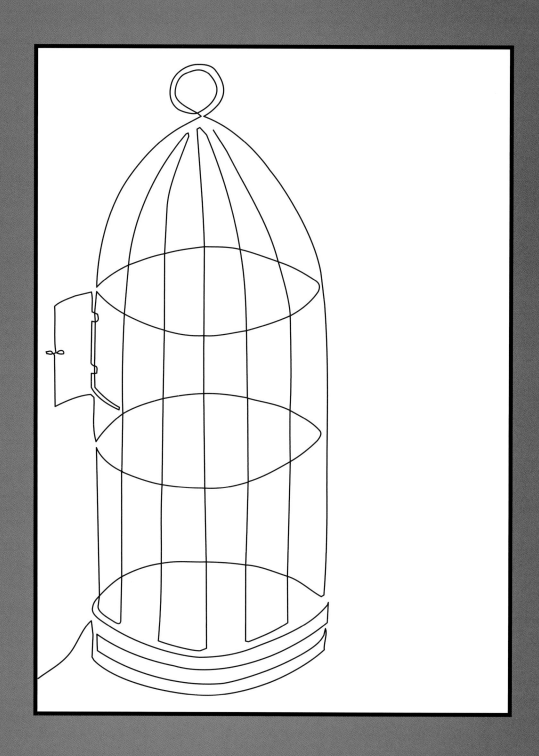

ESCAPE ARTIST

if freedom is nothing more
than being able to choose your own cage
as I suggest it is
then perhaps the fun comes
in being an escape artist

in recognizing the cage you are in
deciding how long you will settle for it
and then
when you want out
seeing how clever you are
at slipping through the wire

then perhaps the good life
the full life
is nothing more
than every once in a while
pulling yourself through a hole
in the roof
standing triumphantly
looking down with a "hot damn!"
and then around
with an "oh shit!"

THE PRISONERS

though I have seen the photographs
of those ragged weary men
still I think I envy them
the prisoners
captured in a good and holy war
which every war has been

caught and confined
by an obviously evil enemy
left to rot
in some forgotten prison camp
stubbornly clinging
to secret information
for which I'd rather die than tell
surviving
in a roach and rat infested cell
my eye fixed
on that thin sliver of hope
at the edge of the door
the crack of light that keeps us alive
in our solitary confinement

yes
there have been times
I've wished it were a simpler prison
for out here
in this open field of sunshine
it is far
far more difficult
to plan the great escape

SCAPEGOAT

what was I doing
conjuring up a scapegoat
when the fact of the matter
was quite sufficient
albeit not as clever and cute

how could I allow myself
to be caught in such an unnecessary lie
helplessly dodging and weaving
trying to rationalize myself
out of this dumb fabrication
this intricate maze of my own making

oh to be Catholic
to slip into the confessional
whispering "Father I lied."
emerging supplied
with a thousand Hail Mary's to do
but not being that kind of believer
there is no place to hide
no place to go except
into the confessional of self
a most unforgiving place

so let the truth be told
and this having been done
the shame will slowly disappear
and I can go to bed and sleep again
not lie awake flagellating myself
for telling such a bold-faced fib

in the grand scheme of things
one's self-esteem is but a grain of sand
yet to the grain of sand
it is all there is

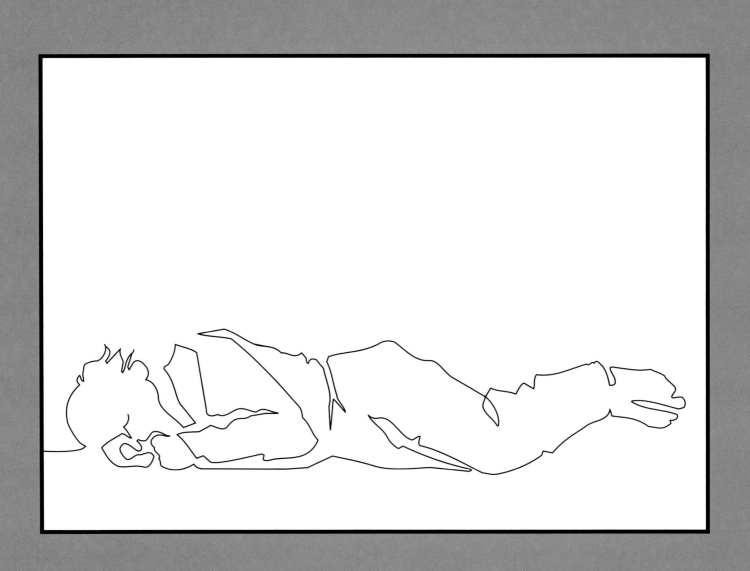

SLEEP

sleep...
recently I have been going to you
as an old fool
to a secret lover
and not unlike a tired salesman
bored with his territory
I have been giving in to temptation
sneaking off in the afternoon
for a quickie little nap
a diversion
always coming out of it with a start
a twinge of fear
telling myself
I shouldn't be here like this
with you

but late in the evening
when the time is right
and what we do together
is socially acceptable
shamelessly
I can give myself to you
completely
forgetting the past
letting the future go
and oh
how I hate to leave you
in the morning

sleep...
you have become an acceptable death
lovers of life — a warning

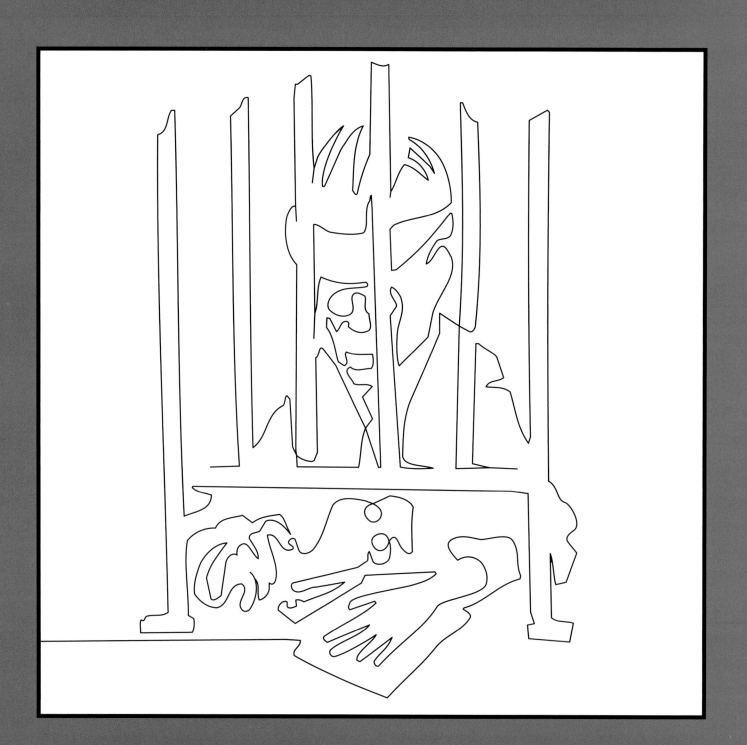

BEFORE MR. HOWARD COMES ALONG, MRS. JAMES

let me say
I have done this long enough to know
that I don't write my poems
we do
and so I live much like
that indistinct little man
in western movies
the one in shirt-sleeves and vest
who seems to exist only at the window
of the telegraph office
never shot — never kissed
his reason for being
simply a gimmick to further the plot

like him I sit at the end of my pen
hunched over sending and receiving
taking the messages down
reading them back to you
and this just came over the wire:

GOOD NEWS   STOP   EVERY HUMAN RELATIONSHIP
THAT HAS EVER BEEN OR WILL EVER BE ENDS   STOP
GOOD NEWS ONLY IF WE USE THE INFORMATION AND
TELL THE PEOPLE WE LOVE THAT WE LOVE THEM AND
DO IT TODAY   STOP   TOMORROW IS ONLY A FIGMENT
OF OUR IMAGINATION STOP   I LOVE YOU
                                                  JESSE

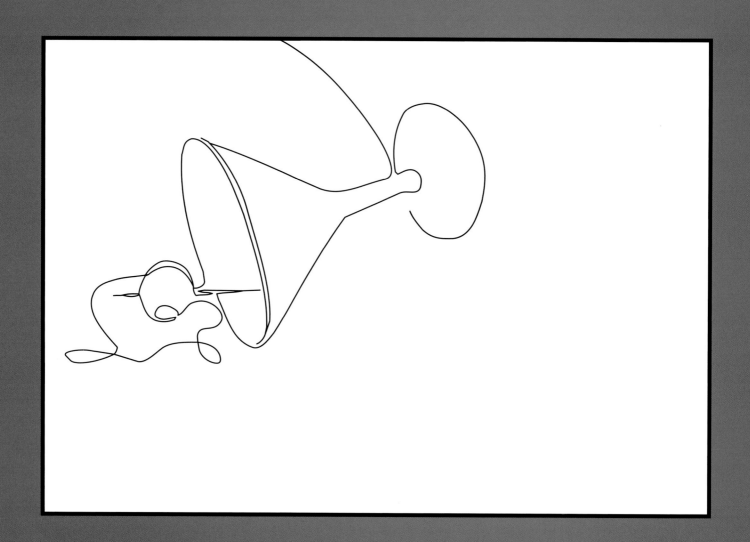

REMEMBERING ALAN

I have been told
that the church will not saint a man
until he's been dead at least fifty years
and that's too bad
for who will be around then
to tell us how he talked too much
and used to pick his nose

now
let me tell about a saint of mine
who not so long ago
was alive and well
and living in California

I had read every word he had written
and could recite his punch lines
like the rosary...
but he was only a writer of books then

he became a saint the night we met
and he was drunk
and fell on the floor vomiting
and...

set me free

ACE

when purchased
it was advertised as one of the first
VWs to migrate to the States and I did develop
a great love for that ugly little green bug
placing it on my affection scale
somewhere between my dog and my wife
and when a prize like this needs servicing
not just any mechanic will do

that's when I heard tell of Ace Bradford
the Volkswagen whisperer
they said all Ace had to do was place
his hands on a skittish bucking motor
and she'd gentle right down and purr
he's brought engines back from the dead
they said and it was true

I drove that VW beetle for decades
inventing reasons to hang out in Ace's garage
watching him work mechanical miracles
enjoying his Southern drawl reminiscent
of cowpokes played by the actor Robert Duvall

in the rear of the shop Ace kept his dreams
bolting them together in his spare time
endurance off-road racing cars
drove them himself – then later with his son
and you should see the trophies they won

years passed, cars came and went
but when I took Ace our new Jeep Cherokee
he grumbled that
he wouldn't be caught dead
staring at a computer screen
wearing a clean white smock
as I left I saw that the dreams
were still there
coming to life in the rear of the shop
after that I lost track of Ace
until I opened the paper
and found him in the obits

now, I'm not a funeral kind of guy
don't like them much at all
but there I was at the funeral hall
and there was Ace
looking like he'd just fallen asleep
I laid my hands on his shoulder
half-expecting his eyelids to flutter open
and give me a wink
but I don't have Ace's magic touch

Clipped his obit – still have it
"Mr. Ace Bradford, died of a heart attack
while participating in a racing event."
about to take first place I'm told
when he slowed – coasting to a stop

as I left the Visitation I thought
"Way to go, Ace!"

WHALES OFF PALO COLORADO

today I saw the whales
moving south along the coast
and had to stop the car and get out
and stand there just watching

one of them came in close to shore
and I thought to myself then
that the whole journey would be worth it
just to see the magic of this Atlantis — rising
blowing and steaming from the sea
an island of life
today I saw the whales
and I was healed

I can tell you now of the dancers
the three girls
and the dark wet highway
and the car
that came hurtling into their young lives
and how the rain fell for five days
as we followed slowly
behind black limousines
three times — slowly — with our lights on

but the sun returned this morning
and the rain has washed the air clean
and brought
the Ventana mountains in so close
they cut my eyes....
sometimes it hurts to see things clearly

for those girls
the dance had just begun
but they went out dancing
trailing veils behind them
and somehow this simple act
tells me that they too paused
somewhere along the way
and saw the whales
moving south along the coast
on a day like today

I hope you will forgive me
for trying to put order and sense to it all
but if I don't, can you tell me
who in hell will?

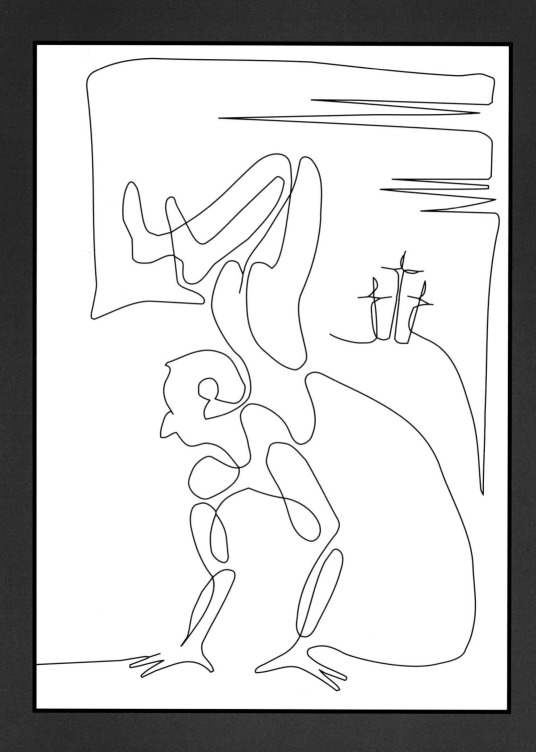

WINDOWS

All night long the rain came down
Left water standing all around.
Muddy puddles on the ground,
Reflect the morning sky.

Down the road there came a man
And he was walking on his hands.
No one seemed to understand
No one even tried to.
And everywhere the stranger goes
People put their chairs in rows.
They sit and listen to his clothes
And no one hears him crying:

"Windows, windows,
Look through those windows
Windows, look into my eyes."

Upside-down he walks the street.
His mental breakdown was complete
Cause when they said:
"Stand on your feet!"
He would ask them: "Why?"
He came by the other day
His quiet eyes did seem to say:
"I will journey all the way,
Out to your horizons."

Windows, windows,
Look through those windows
Windows, look into my eyes

All night long the rain came down
Left water standing all around.
Muddy puddles on the ground,
Reflect the morning sky.

ON THE MOUNTAIN

somewhere about a third of the way up
he came striding down the trail
and caught me unaware
a poet
staff in hand — naked — thin as a whip
wild gray hair framing the sun-stained face
his bright eyes blue holes, the sky showing through

when he saw me resting there
he laughed out loud — "Friend," he said
"I have been to the summit and found nothing
there!
 Absolutely nothing!"
then laughing again he went on down around the
bend
and left me

with my brand-new Day-Glo knapsack
ten-dollar compass and waterproof boots
remembering how I'd sharpened my knife
till it shaved the hair on the back of my wrist
preparing myself for almost anything
but this

still I was young then and it wasn't until I too
had run out of places to climb
that I began to wonder where he was going
and what he was after
laughing that way

so turning around
I followed on down behind
and if I took you by surprise this morning
coming down the path
believe me, I was only laughing at myself
sitting there

THE JUGGLER

it began with oranges
two at first — then more
things naturally swarmed in his hands
and at the grocery store
where he worked as a young man
his head was the sun
and the planets
an egg — a bottle of ketchup
a box of Cornflakes — a jar of jam
and once
when the manager wasn't looking
an eight-and-a-half pound leg of lamb

the bag boys were impressed
and he obsessed now with his own dexterity
threw in a can of soup
a sack of flower — a quart of milk
keeping it up
until he had an entire grocery list
in orbit under control
and then to the imagined drum roll
he would add the single Pringle potato chip

Wow!

and over the years he was not taken out
by the temptation of adding one too many
brussel sprouts and even
when his body was so on top of this juggling act
his mind had time to step aside and ask him
why he was keeping
all that garbage up in the air
he held fast
in the face of that kind of self doubt

he was good all right
really good
but he didn't become great till the night
he dropped everything
except the oranges
which he sat down and ate

HAPPY ENDINGS IN THE BADLANDS

two over-the-hill actors
still play tug of war
with your mask, Kemo Sabe
not that they need the money
they don't
it's just that they won't
give up the tyranny of the dream —
silver bullets and white hats
are hard to let go of —
I know

there's lots of dust and excitement
surrounding the arrival and departure
of the Wells Fargo Stage —
lots of "yeah!" and "ya-hoo!"

however
out near the sixty-mile marker
at a complete standstill
the question arises
who drives the wagon
when ambition and necessity
no longer work for you?
when the grubstake days are over
and you've settled for something less
than being number one
who cracks the whip
and rides shotgun then?

enter the grinning bandito
enter what looks like the end
with pistol in hand and instructions
to "kiss your *culo* good-bye"
and take it from me it's not easy
to keep a positive attitude
with your life
passing before your eyes
but "what the hell" I said to myself
"if this is it, I might as well sit back
and enjoy the show"
which I did and while doing so
caught sight of a pilgrim
who looked a lot like me
doing what he wanted to do
going where he wanted to go
and making a living at it
or more precisely
being paid for the living he made
I mean how lucky can you be?
and with that
the buckboard
was back up to speed

who drives the wagon
when ambition and necessity
no longer work for you?
try gratitude
then cue
the *William Tell Overture*
the Lone Ranger rides again!

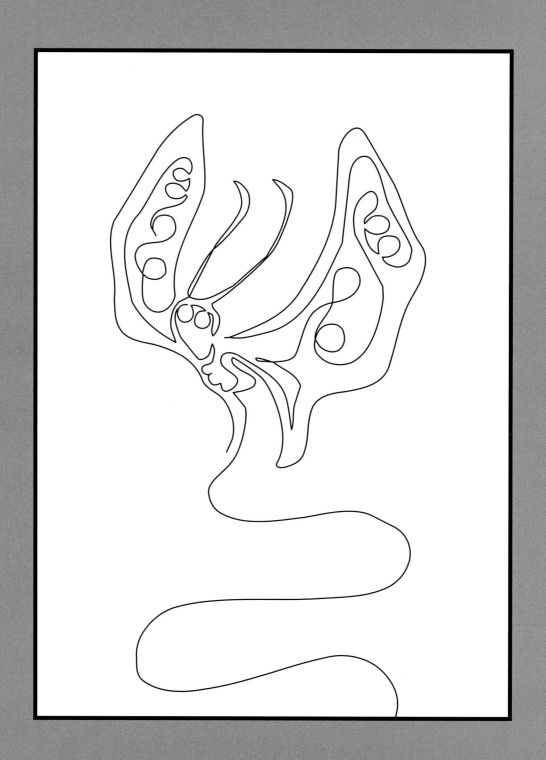

ON BUTTERFLY WINGS

you know for the life of me
I can't recall what happened
last Good Friday...
Christmas I can
because mother got smashed
and the baby seeing his image
distorted
on the surface of a thousand ornaments
cried all day
and on Easter it rained
so that the candy hidden in the grass
got sticky and we had to wash the ants off
before we let the kids out
but somehow I missed Good Friday

looking the other way I guess
like I do
when I pass someone walking the roadside
with an empty gas can
muttering under my breath
about the high cost of funerals
and how the undertakers are bleeding us dry
like vampires
not stopping to realize
that we can't pay those guys enough
to handle what scares us half to death

I mean
if Aunt Maude bites the bag in my kitchen
you're gonna find me outside in the yard
waiting for some weird cat to roll up
in a long black vehicle
and clean up the mess – cart the problem away
smiling all the while

oh
I'll stop by the parlor
Saturday afternoon...
check the flowers out
and have a quick look in the box
but then I never was able to accept
a gift graciously and it's my loss
and no doubt the reason
I sit in my own small house
drinking coffee
feeling homesick most of the time

an old guru once told me
that the only thing
we really have to do in this life is die
and I think I shall repeat this statement
over and over...a hundred times each night
before I go to sleep

perhaps
if I could bring myself to believe it
I mean really believe it
and remember what happens
on Good Friday
I just might come out and find myself
some sunny Easter morning
on butterfly wings
rising!

DANCE BENEDICTION

Yes!
let it be a dance
let life be a dance
because we dance to dance
not to go anywhere
and let it be a dance
let life be a dance
because within the dance
we move easily
with the paradox
knowing
that for every step forward
there must be a step back
and anything else
would have us marching
away from the music